The Question of Meaning

A Theological and Philosophical Orientation

GERHARD SAUTER

Translated and edited by

Geoffrey W. Bromiley

WILLIAM B. EERDMANS PUBLISHING COMPANY
GRAND RAPIDS, MICHIGAN / CAMBRIDGE, U.K.

Originally published 1982 as
Was heisst: nach Sinn fragen? Eine theologisch-
philosophische Orientierung
by Christian Kaiser Verlag, Munich

English translation © 1995 Wm. B. Eerdmans Publishing Co.
255 Jefferson Ave. S.E., Grand Rapids, Michigan 49503 /
P. O. Box 163, Cambridge CB3 9PU U.K.
Printed in the United States of America

00 99 98 97 96 95   7 6 5 4 3 2 1

Library of Congress Cataloging-in-Publication Data

Sauter, Gerhard.
    [Was heisst, nach Sinn fragen? English]
    The question of meaning: a theological and philosophical orientation /
Gerhard Sauter; translated and edited by Geoffrey W. Bromiley.
        p.   cm.
    Includes bibliographical references.
    ISBN 0-8028-0724-0 (alk. paper)
    1. Meaning (Philosophy) — Religious aspects — Christianity. 2. Meaning (Philosophy)
I. Bromiley, Geoffrey William. II. Title.
BR118.S2813 1995
121'.68 — dc20   95-37077
                                                          CIP

Contents

Translator's Preface

READERS of this penetrating study of what is a common issue today should be warned that translation is made more difficult, and the argument harder to follow at some points, by the fact that the German word *Sinn* covers a much broader range than any one English term. When it refers to the five senses one obviously has to use the English "sense," which is also the right word for the so-called sixth sense or the historical or religious sense, and theology has traditionally used "sense" for the natural or allegorical or fourfold sense of Scripture. But when it comes to the *Sinn* of life or act or destiny or experience or suffering, I prefer to use "meaning" or sometimes "purpose," and if the German carries, as it may, the connotation of "mind," one is put in a different sphere in English and the relation to the primary issue may not always be immediately obvious. German also has the advantage of being able to coin different adjectives (or adverbs) more easily with *Sinn,* for example, *sinnvoll* and *sinnhaft,* which cannot be so neatly reproduced in English but which play an important part in Sauter's discussion. I am confident, however, that in spite of these problems the main thrust of the argument emerges clearly enough in the English rendering, and that the result will be a more informed and more circumspect use of the common appeal to the question of meaning, not least in evangelistic and apologetic endeavors.

Santa Barbara   GEOFFREY W. BROMILEY
Lent 1993

Preface

SOME years ago the German railroad had an advertisement that read: "Everybody speaks about the weather, we do not." An advertisement for theology and the church today, but also for many trends in philosophy, sociology, and psychology, might well read: "Everybody speaks about meaning, we do too." The question of meaning was for a time the main topic of a radio program discussing practical philosophy and ethics. It ranks as the decisive religious question in Christian education and in the care of the sick and suffering and dying. But the longer this goes on the more I become convinced that not by a long way does this question bring new life to the question of God, as for many years it was expected to do. I have been forced to conclude that it is really a seeking of idols. I hope that in the process I have not overlooked what is justifiable about it, the way in which it helps our age with the difficulties of orientation. I hope that I have taken adequate account of this contribution. The dubious feature, however, is that the question of meaning usually ends up today being an all-inclusive question. That is the real question which it poses. As in the case of many other questions that by repeated invocation find a niche in our consciousness, we need to ask what the question of meaning itself means.

This work is a revised and expanded version of a prior essay that bore the title "Meaning and Truth."[1] It originated in contributions to

---

1. It was published, essentially unchanged, in the journal *Giornale di Metafisica,*

symposiums[2] and other activities in the years 1977-1982. I am grateful
to the participants in these conversations and discussions, and also to
readers of the essay, for many suggestions and counterquestions that
have helped me to understand this question of meaning. I am particularly grateful to Ingrid Ueberschär of the Kaiser Verlag for her helpful
counsel.

St. Augustine nr. Bonn   GERHARD SAUTER
March 5, 1982

---

n.s. 1 (1979), 245, 292, then in *Evangelische Theologie* 40 (1980), 93, 126 (now out of
print), also in *Religion als Problem der Aufklärung: Eine Bilanz aus der reli-
gionstheoretischen Forschung,* ed. T. Rendtorff (Göttingen, 1980), 69, 106.

2. For example, at a discussion between the editors of *Evangelische Theologie* and
the sociologists N. Luhmann and F. Tenbruck in Bad Homburg on March 14, 1977, also
at a working party on the theory of religion with A. Caracciolo, G. Dux, K. E. Løgstrup,
H. Lübbe, W. Pannenberg, T. Rendtorff, G. Rohrmoser, G. Schmidtchen, and J. Waar-
denburg in Munich on May 25, 1977.

I. THE QUESTION

I READ in a letter that all teachers constantly have the question of meaning in their ears. It is the perspective that catches us up and sets us moving away from the status quo. To many younger people it is an enticing prospect even though they may catch a skeptical note in the question as they put it. The meaning of work, of an obligation, of life itself, will take us beyond all that we have thus far experienced. It makes sense to think along utopian lines because only that which is not yet present can save us. Can it make any sense to rely on a social order that has long since seen its supports decay? For older people the term *meaning* has a different sound. They, too, ask about meaning so as to see where and how things are going. Is not meaning something basic in which they can put their trust and in which they can hide? If so, it makes no sense to burn their bridges behind them and to hazard the good for the sake of something that might be better.

This ambivalence of usage shows us that the more we seek the right approach the greater becomes our uncertainty regarding the direction of all experience and action. Many people find in this uncertainty a crisis of orientation, and they usually equate it with the question of meaning. But the term *meaning* then becomes a chameleon that changes its colors according to the manner of the approach. The two great German political parties have taken up the term into their basic programs in this ultimate form. Thus one of them, while using it sparingly, speaks of "final meaning." People, we read, are seeking self-fulfillment.

They come up against limits. They find that fulfillment lies in a reality above the human world. According to Christian faith, God is the basis of meaning and being. To him we owe life's origin and goal. This insight frees us from the need and the urge to give final meaning to ourselves and to the world. We have the ability and the duty to make moral decisions. We ourselves shape our lives and our world in responsible freedom.[1] God is the basis of meaning and being! Later, precisely in the name of Christian faith, we shall have to question this statement. We must certainly uphold the distinction between receiving meaning and giving it that finds expression above. It is doubtful, however, whether we should mention God, being, and meaning in the same breath. We shall see that the question of meaning, when God is sought as its basis, leads into an abyss.

The other party with its plea for basic values in a threatened world shows itself to be more persuasive, for it addresses the open flank that has produced a progressive and comprehensive demand for meaning. Speaking of the crisis of meaning and anxiety, it says that so long as we had certainty of value-oriented progress, the experiencing of unforeseeable social entanglements was bearable, but with the loss of certainty there have developed fundamental feelings of disorientation and vulnerability. When we no longer know how things will go, we become anxious.[2] Meaning here is thought to be given by the way we shape the world, by work. It is unquestionably this meaning that allows us to set goals and to reach them, but that also creates for us difficulties we simply cannot overcome when we are no longer fully able to see the results of what we do, and productively to agree on what goals we should set. When we find no meaning in the world of work, the question of the meaning of life becomes all the sharper.[3]

Politicians who are pledged to social progress find themselves placed between the generations, or between those who seek meaning as a perspective that catches them up and all the others who want to find

1. Draft of a platform for the Christian Democratic Union of Germany proposed by the platform commission in *CDU-Grundsatzdiskussion: Beiträge aus Wissenschaft und Politik,* ed. R. von Weizsäcker, Goldmann Sachbuch 11191 (1977), 247ff., quoting from 247.

2. *Theorie und Grundwerte: Grundwerte in einter gefährdeten Welt,* recommended by the Grundwerte-Kommission to the SPD leaders, 1977, 4.

3. Ibid.

solid ground again under their feet. But they are all necessarily brought together at the point where a world of unlimited possibilities is already a thing of the past. Thus in a comparison of politics, ethics, and religion we read that socially the question of meaning unites all those who want to bring in a new world in the name of scientific and technological progress. The question of meaning is no longer a private question but a political question, a question of decision.[4] It is a political question because it is a political matter when a crisis of meaning develops that can no longer deny its social and political origins. Even now, however, there is doubt as to whether answers, final answers, can be given to the question of meaning. The Social Democrat Commission on Basic Values certainly maintains that the state cannot mediate or posit such answers.[5] Nevertheless, it can create conditions for a free exchange of questions and answers regarding the crisis of meaning.[6] It can thus guarantee a kind of free market for values and goals, even those of a religious nature.

Crisis of meaning, question of meaning, giving of meaning — these are some examples of the combinations with the term *meaning* that we find today. The term occurs in many connections, all of which take for granted that the term's own meaning is plain. Thus we read of its content, of meaningfulness, of the constitution and interpretation of meaning, of finding it, of establishing it, of confidence in it, and of the meaning of suffering or life or history. It is not the fault of the term that concepts so different from one another come together in relation to it. For example, the German term *(Sinn)* occurs in a negative sense in the words for "nonsense," "contradiction," and "meaninglessness" *(Unsinn, Widersinn, Sinnlosigkeit)*, but what do these really have in common? An American publication can speak of "working with values" and the German translator renders this as *Sinnfindung*.[7] A linguistic artifice makes of the elementary task of directing action with the help of values and goals an all-embracing problem of orientation by which

4. R. Reitz, "Was ist das 'Ethische' an der SPD? Anmerkungen zum Sebstverständnis von Christen in der SPD," *Sozialdemokratischer Informationsdienst: Kirchenfragen, evangelischer Bereich* (August 1980), 38ff., quoting from 38.

5. *Theorie und Grundwerte*, 15.

6. Ibid.

7. L. E. Raths, M. M. Harmin, and S. B. Simon, *Values and Teaching: Working with Values in the Classroom* (Columbus, Ohio, 1966).

human existence stands or falls. We can obviously accept the relation to values and norms only if the impression is given that the questions we face are final and comprehensive or that a loss of values is again to be made good.

All these associations seem to be covered by the question of meaning, but they do not tell us by a long way why or in what sense we are asking about meaning or how far meaning itself can be a question. The question of meaning becomes an expression for all kinds of unrest, of disruptions of life, of feelings that there is no way out. But when the question is on so many lips as it now seems to be, it is time to ask more precisely why meaning is supposed to be in doubt.[8] It might be that with the question a soap bubble ascends that glistens so confusingly because problems of orientation reflect themselves in it. The word *meaning* needs to be clarified. Before putting questions of meaning and trying to answer them, we must stop for a moment and explore the semantic field of the term itself to see whether the question of meaning is really so intrinsically human as it is unthinkingly taken to be today. Has it perhaps arisen in specific conditions, in a constellation that we must examine in order not to come under its spell or to deliver ourselves up to it?

8. For a helpful essay on this investigation with good examples, also from contemporary literature, see the little study by E. Feil, "Zum Sinn der Sinnfrage," *Stimmen der Zeit* 195 (1977), 3ff.

II. THE SENSES, SENSE, AND MEANING

I
T IS only recently that "meaning" has become so ambivalent. This applies especially to the German term *Sinn* and the English *sense*. Former generations did not use the term in the extended way we do today. In German the original reference was to perception, especially spatial, that is, looking in a certain direction,[1] and therefore moving toward something.[2]

The Latin *sentire* meant to follow a direction.[3] The French *sens* ("direction") retains this meaning. Linguistically comparable is the Gothic *sinpan*, "to go," and the Old High German *sinnan*, "to travel, go, strive."[4] The article on *Sinn* in the German dictionary of the brothers Grimm[5] adduces many meanings, but common to all of them is the thought of orientation even and especially in the intellectual sphere, that is, in that of consciousness. This meaning, which is predominant in the Latin *sensus*

1. J. and W. Grimm, *Deutsches Wörterbuch*, vol. X/1 (Leipzig, 1905), 1103.

2. W. Weier, *Sinn und Teilhabe: Grundproblem der abendländischen Geistesentwicklung* (Munich, 1970), 21.

3. F. Kluge and A. Götze, *Etymologisches Wörterbuch der deutschen Sprache*, 15th ed. (Berlin, 1951), 726.

4. J. E. Heyde, "Vom Sinn des Wortes Sinn, Prolegomena zu einer Philosophie des Sinnes," in *Sinn und Sein: Ein philosophisches Symposion*, ed. R. Wisser (Tübingen, 1960), 70.

5. Grimm, *Deutsches Wörterbuch*, X/1, 1103; and cf. H. Paul, *Deutsches Wörterbuch* (Halle, 1897), 418f.

(although it developed independently of the German usage), relates always to perception and modes of perception. In New High German *Sinn* is the organ of perception, and in the plural this is the main sense.[6] Within the semantic field are many transitions that defy close demarcation and make it hard to trace the historical development. It is the more surprising, then, that today when the question of meaning is raised in Germany, *Sinn* has been detached from the concept of perception or the plain relation to perception.[7] The Grimm article traces usage only up to the first half of the nineteenth century and hence gives no examples of how this change took place. This fact supports my own conjecture that the question of meaning is of recent origin.

Though orientation or the directing of perception is not the only meaning of *Sinn*, it is still a common one today. And we find it similarly in the English *sense*. Thus we speak of the five senses that we all need to have. Those who can say they have a sixth sense are claiming that they can detect what is above and outside nature, though we may perhaps simply say that they are not normal. In a transferred sense we also speak of a further sense, sometimes called a seventh sense, which those who drive automobiles today need to cultivate as a kind of looking ahead and around, an awareness of possible eventualities. Sensing means moving out of oneself even and precisely where the totality of intellectual perception is indicated. Jost Trier in his study *Der deutsch Wortschatz im Sinnbezirk des Verstandes* has shown that *sin* originally was a term for our inborn rational side[8] and equivalent to sagacity relative to the world, the ability to comprehend the world and to encounter it with skill. The understanding, then, is not just receptive but also itself active. It can imagine meaning as it ponders and thinks.[9] But its reference is still to perception. Tension thus arises that can lead to the intellectual venture of making meaning independent of perceptions. This may well be the background of the express search for meaning.

"Sense" or "meaning" is also communicated perception. Here we

---

6. Grimm, *Deutsches Wörterbuch*, X/1, 1138.

7. The situation differs in English, since "meaning" rather than "sense" is the preferred term for the question. — TRANS.

8. J. Trier, *Der deutsche Wortschatz im Sinnbezirk des Verstandes: Die Geschichte eines sprachlichen Feldes*, vol. I (Heidelberg, 1931), 300.

9. Grimm, *Deutsches Wörterbuch*, X/1, 1136.

have it in a treated form. It is oriented to the receptive reason that itself stands in need of speech. Linguistic sense is midway between sign and interpretation. F. L. G. Frege in his treatise *Sinn und Bedeutung* (1892), which laid a foundation for the development of linguistic logic, defined this midway position as that of a regular link to the sign, whose sense and interpretation are of such a kind that the sign has a specific sense to which a specific interpretation belongs, but the latter, which is the object, may also have other signs. The one meaning may have different terms for it in different languages or even in the same language.[10] As a linguistic pointer or as perception by way of speech, as the meaning of a term, phrase, or text, "sense" or "meaning" has become the quintessence of understanding and agreement. The German *Sinn* can also come to denote a thought, especially one that is succinctly and pregnantly formulated, a sentence, or an epigram. Thus, from the seventeenth century onward, thoughts expressed in this way have been called in German *Sinngedichte,* as in F. von Logau's collection *Deutscher Sinn-Gedichte* (1654). A later epigrammatist required that sentences of this kind be meaningful, not in the sense that they have to have the probing profundity that some suspect in them, but simply in the sense that they cannot come from blockheads with neither sense nor understanding.[11] This German usage clearly preserves the link to the first basic meaning.

Is there more to say about the connection between linguistic sense and the senses? Is not language itself and as a whole — quite apart from the specific sense and meaning of a sign — a sensory picture, a mysterious web of relations forming the world which encloses us and out of which we cannot fall? Thus linguistic philosophers like J. G. Herder and W. von Humboldt saw in speech an instrument that we forge, or rather the basic instrument that enables us to use the senses on behalf of our human world.

But as "sense" seems to find a home in this way in speech, it undergoes a decisive change in its own field of meaning and experiences incalculable expansion. It now comes to indicate all that which we find to be significant for us. This is the hermeneutical meaning of "sense."

---

10. F. L. G. Frege, "Sinn und Bedeutung" (1892), in *Funktion, Begriff, Bedeutung: Fünf logische Studien,* ed. G. Patzig (Göttingen, 1962), 40.

11. C. Wernicke, *Überschriften* (1763), quoted in "Sinngedicht," *Deutsches Wörterbuch,* X/1, 1177.

We have to remember that Christian theology not least of all prepared the way for this understanding. From the first it was asking what is the *sensus* of Holy Scripture, first of the Hebrew Bible, which has a different meaning for Christian faith from that for Jewish piety, then for the texts that were written in the days of the primitive church. One might suppose that all that was sought was the actual sense or meaning of the text, the sense of the words and sentences that found different expression in the various traditions. But according to some views of early church exposition of the Bible, the *sensus,* being related to faith, is accompanied by a special perception that discloses this meaning. Naturally, as was emphasized, this perception has nothing whatever to do with the senses and the sensory world. On the contrary, it derives from the Spirit of God, who causes us to understand what God has communicated to us in the words of our own language. On the basis of what Paul says about the letter killing and the Spirit giving life (2 Cor. 3:6), Origen at the beginning of the third century was the first to speak of a spiritual sense *(sensus spiritualis)* in contrast to the mere literal sense *(sensus literalis).* In this way the sense was again closely related to the means of perception. The perception of faith that is directed by the Spirit of God — though it might not be called this — is a sensing of the true sense *(Sinn für den Sinn)* of the text. Without the Spirit the sense would be subject to our natural perception and would be no more than mere hairsplitting devoid of real meaning.[12]

The later developed theory of a multiple sense of Scripture, to which we shall return, gave the biblical texts a context of meaning both above and before it on which the meaning of each individual word and sentence depends. To ask what is the meaning of a biblical text is thus to consider what is its meaning for faith. The response of the text is directed by faith. It is true that this faith cannot exist without the biblical Word. Nevertheless, the text can say only what the Spirit of faith recognizes. A shift has taken place here. The sense of the words or sentences is

12. Origen, *De principiis* 50.1.2. Origen here contrasts the corporeal and the intellectual or spiritual, and applies the contrast to that of life and death made by Paul in 2 Cor. 3:6 within both humans and the world (Die Griechischen christlichen Schriftsteller 22:18). In *Contra Celsum* 106.70 (Die Griechischen christlichen Schriftsteller 3:140), in exposition of 2 Cor. 3:6, the literal exposition is sensory and the spiritual is "intelligible," while in *Contra Celsum* 7.20 (Die Griechischen christlichen Schriftsteller 3:171f.), the linguistic level is distinguished from the sphere of understanding.

subordinated to a total sense that decides the meaning of the specific sense. This spiritual total sense has to maintain itself vis-à-vis other dimensions of meaning. It stands over against the literal sense and may even be opposed to it.

But here we have only forerunners of the "sense" or "meaning" that we speak of today. So long as meaning was regarded as something given to us by perception, as a thought or as the statement of a text, it had a specific and limited sense when any question was raised. What was in view was the meaning of a statement or text or the meaning found by an individual. Today, however, the question is that of meaning in an absolute sense. Sense does not just stand opposed to nonsense, as in expounding a text or examining thoughts and statements. The alternative is meaninglessness.

The nineteenth-century history of the German term *Sinn* seems to me to give evidence of this momentous change. It was only at this period that the term took on the absolute and dubious significance that is important for most of us today and that most of us find so oppressive. To the meanings sketched thus far we now need to add three more that quickly began to push the earlier ones into the background.

Sense is first the relation of an action or statement to what is intended. We have here still the idea of a direction that was intrinsic to sensing as perception. But now "sense" has become the substance of a text or statement. We are asking what is the point of life, action, or speech. It is only along these lines that we can understand expressions like "the meaning of life," "the meaning of work," or "the meaning of suffering."

In thus taking on its own life the term then came to mean the same as "purpose," and above all "value." Fundamental here is the idea that the world of things does not (or not yet) coincide with what is decisive for our experiences and actions. What is said in human life, even in the form of its acts, is not the same as what is normatively intended in it. So long as facts and goals clash with one another, the question of meaning arises, the meaning of specific experiences and actions as well as that of life as a whole, the ultimate meaning from which all that is penultimate receives its relative value. Value philosophy in particular has adopted this mode of inquiry and thus uses terms like "finding meaning" or "giving meaning."[13] It is no accident that this philosophical

13. As I see it, there is no adequate terminology clarification. H. Münsterberg,

trend with its concern for world orientation comes to the surface in times of crisis, as after World Wars I and II and in the later twentieth century.

Finally the term denotes the comprehensive context, the sustaining totality, when phenomena, actions, or texts are integrated into their full relations. This meaning finds emphatic expression in terms like "context

---

Philosophie der Werte, Grundzüge einer Weltanschauung (Leipzig, 1908; 2nd ed. 1921), p. v, says that the question of meaning and interpretation leads to the world of values and plays a role in the search for a view of life and the world. J. K. Holzamer, "Der Begriff des Sinnes, entwickelt im Anschluss an das 'irreale Sinngebilde' bei Heinrich Rickert" (diss., Munich, 1929), derives the understanding of *Sinn* from Kant's view of transcendental apperception as an explanation of meaning that cannot be understood psychologically and links this explanation of meaning to a given factor that must be seen as a structure and intentionality of the soul that in some way anticipates and reflects the real world (58). Sense understanding is nonsensory. See also R. Eucken, *Der Sinn und Wert des Lebens* (Leipzig, 1908; 9th ed. 1922); ET *The Meaning and Value of Life* (repr. London, 1916); H. Gomperz, *Über Sinn und Sinngebilde, Verstehen und Erklären* (Tübingen, 1929); G. Ralfs, *Sinn und Sein im Gegenstande der Erkenntnis* (Tübingen, 1931); N. Hartmann, "Sinngebung und Sinnerfüllung," *Blätter für deutsche Philosophie* 8 (1934), 1-38; idem, *Zur Grundlegung der Ontologie* (Berlin and Leipzig, 1935); P. Hofmann, *Sinn und Geschichte: Historisch-systematische Einleitung in die sinn-erforschende Philosophie* (Munich, 1937); also *Problem und Probleme einer Sinn-erforschenden Philosophie,* ed. K. Hamburger (Stuttgart, 1980); W. Burkamp. *Wirklichkeit und Sinn,* 2 vols. (Berlin, 1938); H. Rikkert, *Unmittelbarkeit und Sinndeutung: Aufsätze zur Ausgestaltung des Systems der Philosophie* (Tübingen, 1939); R. Bechert, *Eine Sinnphilosophie im Grundriss dargestellt* (Munich, 1941); F.-J. von Rintelen, "Sinn und Sinnverständnis," *Zeitschrift für philosophische Forschung* 2 (1947), 69ff. For a good survey cf. H. Rehfeld, "Sinn und Wert: Das Problem des Bedeutungsverhältnisses von Sinnverständnis und Wertbewusstsein . . . und seine Lösung als Versuch einer metaphysischen Grundlegung der Wertlehre" (diss., Berlin, 1954). In this discussion we have a mix of epistemology, ontology, the philosophy of culture, and phenomenology (esp. in M. Scheler, who investigates the inner sense psychologically and relations and unions of meaning phenomenologically from the standpoint of filling with meaning and motivating conduct). As regards the philosophy of culture cf. E. Spranger, *Lebenserfahrungen* (Tübingen and Stuttgart, 1945), 30f.: "A true human life is a constant search for the supreme value or final meaning in terms of which life is to be seen." Convictions of this type strongly influenced postwar pedagogy; see A. Roder, "Die Sinnfrage als pädagogisches Problem: Versuch einer kulturpädagogischen Besinnung" (diss., Tübingen, 1955). For a study of "concept" from the standpoint of a philosophy of values cf. R. Lauth, *Die Frage nach dem Sinn des Daseins* (Munich, 1953), esp. 28f., 32, 34. For Lauth the basic philosophical functions of the concept of meaning cover constitutive arranging, interpreting, and offering purpose and value.

of meaning" or "totality of meaning." These expressions indicate that the detail can receive its meaning only from the whole and can thus be posited only in the light of the whole.[14] In the absolute, then, "meaning" is a category of reality. To ask about meaning is no less than to ask about what is real. If we cannot find an answer to this question, there is no longer anything to which we can really cling. We have fallen out of the world and are groping in the void. The question of meaning has thus become a question of being or nonbeing.

It has *become* this, we must stress. Human history has undoubtedly always seen and will always see experiences of futility, times of basic doubt, crises of orientation. But between these and the question of meaning that has been with us for the last century and a half there is a gap. We cannot leap over this gap by reading back our problems into older testimonies to the search for meaning. We shall not be open to Job and Old Testament skepticism, to the philosophers of antiquity responding to shattering events in their time, to mystics in the autumn of the Middle Ages, or to doubters in the dawn of the modern era, if all we catch in them is an echo — an echo of the crisis of meaning that is experienced by a disillusioned belief in progress or face-to-face with a world of work that no longer communicates to us the meaning that we ascribe to it. Answers that were previously given to the questions of meaning will no longer speak to us so long as we do not pay attention to the uniqueness of these questions and measure our own questions by them. We have to begin, then, at the gap that separates the absolute question of meaning from all that went before.

The history of the term can form an important starting point. In contrast to older fields of meaning a concept emerged in the nineteenth century that can cover previous usage as well. Meaning is achieved by a process of interrelating. This will make possible a new and comprehensive understanding of perception, thought, and language. To earlier meanings are now added those that do not merely embrace new fields

14. W. Pannenberg has adopted this perspective. He differentiates a referential, intentional, and contextual understanding of meaning and tries to connect them in a theory of the integration of all modes of perception (*Theology and the Philosophy of Science* [ET Philadelphia, 1976], 206ff.); cf. also M. Müller, "Über Sinn und Sinnge-fahrdung des menschlichen Daseins," *Philosophisches Jahrbuch* 74 (1966/67), 4: "absolute meaning as the self-meaning of the totality of life and its world."

but do more. They reach beyond the world of direct experience and soar up to a point where there can be a survey of the day-to-day and all its relations can be made plain.

Historical meaning, a sense of history, promises to do this. By tying together various data and their causes and effects it teaches us to understand afresh the world in which we live, and to see it especially as a nexus of human modes of expression. Or it might be speech, as we have already said, that will serve as an instrument of human life in the world, as a creative general sense that embraces all that happens to humanity, making a hostile, puzzling, and often disconnected world around us into a world for us. Or religion might prove to be, as F. Schleiermacher once called it, a "sense [*Sinn*] and taste for the Infinite."[15] This sounds as though a further sense were added to our five senses in religious experience, and that this sense, like the others, enables us to perceive or taste something. But "taste" also denotes the power of aesthetic judgment that will grasp the infinite but cannot comprehend it. In religious feeling we can measure all that is finite in its relation to the infinite. The religious sense is not really a sixth sense, an instrument by which to perceive what is supersensory. Only in metaphorical exaggeration is it a higher sense. It is really the sense of all senses, an integrating center that enables us to move above ourselves and in this way to become whole. Finally, religious feeling also embraces the meaning of the biblical texts. In order to understand these texts, it has to be creatively active, and since it is in direct contact with the infinite, why should it not, at least occasionally, be itself creative and produce its own new texts? That is what Schleiermacher meant logically. He was not in this way abandoning the question of the meaning of Scripture but expanding its scope.

Here, then, we have some provisional examples of the basic change of meaning that we must keep in view if we are to understand the question of meaning and its development. If instead we were to plunge at once into the question of meaning as it now confronts us, we would not be able, as I see it, to give any truly comprehensive answer to our real question: What does it mean to ask about meaning? For the way of speaking about meaning today no longer shows awareness of the controlling conditions under which this way of speaking developed. As a

15. F. D. E. Schleiermacher, *On Religion* (ET New York, 1968), 39.

rule the question of meaning takes it for granted that "meaning" means gaining mastery over life. The answer to the question that is expected, then, is one that will help us to control existence even if it has nothing very palpable to offer. There is confidence that meaning can govern human action. This relation to action is the leading thought in most understandings of meaning in current usage. In keeping with this, specific actions may be said to interpret or to give or to establish meaning. The result is that what is to be shown is no longer, for example, the meaning of a specific act, for it is the meaning of action in general that seems to be in question. Again, what is at issue is the meaning of work and not just of a specific activity that has become problematical. Again, the meaning of life is put in such a way that life itself now seems to be something that we have to bring forth. In short, meaning in the absolute is needed if we are to be able to live. This is what it now means to ask about meaning.

But is "meaning" in this complex sense as a mastering of life itself a part of human life? Are we sick if we lack meaning in this sense? Does health suffer if we even ask about meaning? Or is the question of meaning a sign of vitality, of the will to live? Opinions about this differ among those who have made the mastering of life their special study. For example, Freud found in the question of meaning an expression of soul sickness: The moment we ask about the meaning and value of life we are sick.[16] We are no longer in harmony with natural life, which, as Freud saw it, is a nexus of psychological forces whose rules we must control and can discern. Jung, however, called neurosis the suffering of the soul that has not found its meaning.[17] In this case the psyche is naturally searching for meaning because it can find rest and refuge only in a totality that embraces all specific things, even specific human powers. As other theoreticians of the life of the soul begin with hunger or power or impulse to explain the life of living creatures and to find a basis for human existence, Jung, and even more emphatically Frankl, trace back what is specifically human to the search for meaning. Meaning is the nourishment of the spirit. It is thus the decisive food for

16. S. Freud, *Briefe* (1873) (1939; repr. Frankfurt, 1960), 429, quoted by U. Böschemeyer, *Die Sinnfrage in Psychotherapie und Theologie: Die Existenzanalyse und Logotherapie Viktor E. Frankls aus theologischer Sicht* (Berlin and New York, 1977), 16n.4.

17. C. G. Jung, "Psychotherapists or the Clergy," in *Psychology and Religion: East and West,* vol. 11 of *Collected Works* (ET London, 1958), 330-31.

humanity, for we humans are fundamentally spirits that have to grasp the world as a whole if we are to be able to exist in it.

Perhaps we have here important differences between psychological schools that rest on different philosophical presuppositions. For example, Frankl realized how indebted he was to the values philosopher Max Scheler.[18] What counts decisively, however, is something in common that brings them all back together, namely, their therapeutic view of humanity as a life-fulfillment. Although Frankl does not understand psychotherapeutic assistance as a technique, it is he who makes this point most explicitly. One of his main works deals with the human search for meaning.[19] The question struck home to him in the concentration camp, where survival was specifically a matter of the spirit having confidence in the ultimate meaning of existence. In this light Frankl came to see that we cannot exist, let alone survive, unless existence has meaning. The meaning of existence underlies every expression of life, every action, not just special outreaching efforts, but precisely the acts that are totally elementary, and it still does so even when we despair of the future and put an end to life. Exactly at that point our act stands related to a whither, in this case to death, which bears a definite relation to life. It thus gives evidence in an extreme form that we live by an openness that compels us to ask about meaning. As Frankl says more precisely, we do not become aware of meaning in the absolute, the meaning of the cosmic totality, when we take leave of our present existence. We achieve awareness of the meaning of existence that sustains us and the whole world only in the concreteness of the situation in which we move and come face-to-face with those who relate to us and we to them. This meaning is reality as a whole, yet not reality in the abstract, but what is also to be grasped. What is there for us has to be viewed by us in this fact of its being there. Only thus does the given meaning of reality, reality as the *logos* of being, correspond to the meaning that is found by us in virtue of our spirit. Only thus do the fact of meaning and its discovery correspond. To find meaning is not to fall out of the world. That the world is sustained, that meaning is established

18. Böschemeyer, *Sinnfrage*, 1, 19ff.

19. V. I. Frankl, *Der Mensch auf der Suche nach Sinn: Zur Rehumanisierung der Psychotherapie*, 2nd ed. (Stuttgart, 1973). ET of 1st ed.: *Man's Search for Meaning* (Boston, 1970).

for it, is something that always, even when we do not say so, we pre-suppose in our lives when we act. But life and action can still fail to see meaning even though they are naturally oriented to it. The world may seem to be an incoherent conglomeration, a confusion of accidents with no discernible linkage. Then we experience a lack of meaning, the sick-ness of spirit that can finally be healed only when the basic meaning of reality — Frankl's supermeaning[20] — embraces the spirit.

This is how the search for meaning becomes the quest for God, for God is the name for this superworld[21] that gives meaning to our world. To come up against God is as it were the most natural thing in the world when the part of life that is the search for meaning presses on to the end. That it should do so is not, of course, self-evident. A weakness of society, and especially of Western culture in our time, is that we quickly see symptoms of deficiency of the will for meaning and its expression in experiences of meaninglessness. In diagnosis the psychotherapist becomes a critic of culture who uncovers the pathology of a society that is alienated from the *logos*. What can be offered by way of healing? We cannot force this society to engage in the quest for God, but we may perhaps suggest plausibly that healing will come if it searches for mean-ing, that this search will be an important step in the healing process. Religion is then a dimension of therapy even if not everyone can attain to it and even if fewer still can use it to help others. Many helpful steps can be taken to reach this dimension, and they have to be taken if the human spirit is to have the room it needs to live.

It is perhaps true that what Frankl and, even more so, many of his disciples offer is a secular idea of healing, and the fluidity of the tran-sition from this mode of healing to religious interpretations of meaning supports that idea. For this reason many psychotherapeutic practices are linked almost without a break to symbols that depict the relations of meaning between the everyday and the superworld, for example, the healing process of self-acceptance oriented to the life of Jesus, who has

20. Frankl, *Ärztliche Seelsorge,* 8th ed. (Vienna, 1971), 44. ET of 1st ed.: *The Doctor and the Soul* (New York, 1955; 3rd ed. 1986), 32-33.
21. Ibid.; and idem, *Der Wille zum Sinn* (Bern, Stuttgart, and Vienna, 1972), 117; ET *The Will to Meaning,* expanded ed. (New York, 1988), 144-45; here Frankl asks whether we do not have to assume that the human world itself and for its part is transcended by a world inaccessible to us whose meaning or suprameaning alone can give meaning to our suffering.

ended all tensions between the self and the world, and also within the self, by his relationship with God that symbolized completed reconciliation.[22] We find another example of interpretation of meaning as an aid to life in the ethical debate concerning the meaning of work. All work appears to be meaningful because and to the extent that it participates in the creative work of God that transcendently directs all historical constructs to the goal of consummation in the kingdom of God. Thus Jürgen Moltmann says that if we want a comprehensive concept for the meaning of work for individuals and society it lies close to hand in the idea of working for the kingdom of God. This idea can indicate the eschatological meaning of all work and of society itself as it historically adjusts to nature. The world is not complete. By work we may take part in destroying the world or in preserving it. We work not only with the God who creates but also with the God who redeems.[23]

The symbiosis of the mastering of life and religion, however, is not decisive in explanation of the question of meaning. We may have many objections to the giving of meaning along such lines. We may say that strictly the mastering of life is not possible because it ascribes to us a power we do not have, or that we can experience it only in a way that makes it appear effortless. This is not, however, the crucial point. What counts is the question of the meaning that sustains life even in all its vulnerability and incomprehensibility, even with all its riddles, when we can expect from it a representation of the sheltering reality and all-embracing totality. The search for meaning in the various expressions of life and modes of action is no other than the search for the healing power that promises to reunite a divided world. A therapy of meaning involves arranging things in such a way as to establish relations, or at least to discover them again when they have vanished. In this form the question of meaning seems to be a healing one because it constantly strides ahead and nowhere calls a halt. It is here that many experts find its religious power.

The expansion of the question of meaning, however, leads to a progressive reduction of the perception of what it is that gives form to life. Perception is restricted to interpretation, to finding the meaning

22. Jung, "Psychotherapists or the Clergy," 334f.
23. J. Moltmann, "Der Sinn der Arbeit," in *Recht und Arbeit — Sinn der Arbeit,* ed. Moltmann (Munich, 1979), 81f.

and significance whose network of relations individuals or human societies know how to rule and handle. Instead of being caught in this
network, everything new that is encountered can apparently be brought
into it. This procedure is a reduction and fateful restriction because it
knows meaning only as the opposite of meaninglessness and contradiction. Everything is always at risk: Those who have no ground under
them fall out of the world. Those who are not healthy, or at least on the
way to health in the search for meaning, are incurably sick.

The process of reduction carries with it the supposedly radical or
absolute question of meaning. This question is so fascinating just because it promises to describe and comprehend everything that meets us
in our world. It does not always take the form of speculative reflection
on the total meaning of the world. An expert on the soul like Frankl
has noted that that kind of reflection is beyond us and can cause psychological harm. Even so, Frankl did not have in view the limited meaning of specific actions but the antithesis of sense and nonsense as this
comes to expression in experience and action. The finding of meaning
at each moment of life is not, then, a purely intellectual task. On the
contrary, those who assume that no one can exist without meaning have
to see the question of meaning arising even in elementary actions, but
especially do we seek and find meaning where we communicate with
one another, where we reach agreement by various kinds of signs and
achieve fellowship in the medium of speech.

That the question of meaning is everywhere present is something
which those disciplines try to show that study and establish the conditions of human existence, how the world is constructed for us, how we
are shaped in our dealings with it. For such disciplines mastering life is
not just a theoretical matter. They themselves are part of the venture.
They try to make it possible and even more successful by explaining the
hidden processes of establishing meaning. Here the intellectual thrust
that the term *meaning* seems to have for many people today becomes a
matter of method. We have referred already to psychology and its ad-
vocacy of the healing power of meaning. Alongside it, and often in
competition with it as an explanation of the world, sociology has found
in meaning a basic category of social action[24] and proposed a whole

24. For one of the most important modern contributions cf. N. Luhmann, "Sinn
als Grundbegriff der Soziologie," in Habermas and Luhmann, *Theorie der Gesellschaft*

series of reconstructions to try to make the history of the world's development intelligible in a shifting sequence of conceptions of reality.[25] For such studies the theory of speech as a system of signs (semiotics) seems well adapted to explain the development of our human world, the growing of individuals into the reality that confronts them and that achieves no reality without their cooperation, whether in a palpable way, in one that can be apprehended in speech, or in one that expresses itself intellectually.[26] We must also refer to the older tradition of understanding meaning, that is, hermeneutics.[27] Once this was just a matter of finding a theory of textual exposition by way of understanding speech, but in the twentieth century it has come to involve the understanding of reality in terms of speech. With its universal claim it contests the corresponding self-understanding of sociology and psychology and allies itself with the philosophical trends already mentioned that relate meaning to being. Here, then, is the stately phalanx of disciplines that in spite of their inner controversies are all concerned about the sustaining role of meaning and about global meaning.

If I myself begin to ask about meaning along different lines than those depicted it is because the reduction of perception to the interpretation and establishment of meaning does not leave play for the multiplicity of the modes of perception. That perception is also orientation is lost, too, if meaning involves only taking action to arrange things, to relate subjects to objects, phenomena to a total view, and so on. This understanding simply confirms the image of our society as a sick one because it stands in need of meaning. To show this, and to make way for other perceptions, I have to look at the usage in other

---

oder Sozialtechnologie — Was leistet die Systemforschung? (Frankfurt, 1971), 25ff. Cf. on this E. Herms, "Das Problem von 'Sinn als Grundbegriff der Soziologie' bei Niklas Luhmann," *Zeitschrift für Evangelische Ethik* 18 (1974), 341ff., reprinted in Herms, *Theorie für die Praxis-Beiträge zur Theologie* (Munich, 1982), 189ff.

25. On this cf. G. Dux, *Die Logik der Weltbilder: Sinnstrukturen im Wandel der Geschichte* (Frankfurt, 1982).

26. For an inquiry along the lines of a theory of development cf. E. V. Clark, *The Ontogenesis of Meaning,* Linguistische Forschungen 27 (Wiesbaden, 1979).

27. E. Betti, *Die Hermeneutik als allgemeine Methodik der Geisteswissenschaften* (Tübingen, 1962); idem, *Allgemeine Auslegungslehre als Methodik des Geisteswissenschaften* (Tübingen, 1967); H. G. Gadamer, *Wahrheit und Methode,* 2nd ed. (Tübingen, 1965), 361ff.; ET *Truth and Method* (New York, 1988), 274ff.

disciplines that are oriented to meaning. I do not want to examine the concept but to pursue inquiries that might help us to recognize that meaning is a questionable thing in a positive as well as a negative sense. In chapter III we will first come up against the different senses of "meaningful" that we must advance to reach a theological decision. Then the question of action and meaning in chapter IV will lead us to sociology, and in contrast we must consider the contributions of the philosophy of history in chapter V, and religious theory, psychology, and social philosophy in chapter VI. Finally we shall have to take up specifically theological problems relating to the understanding of meaning: the meaning of Scripture, the understanding of the Bible in recent New Testament studies, and the relation of both to total meaning (chap. VII). On the basis thus laid down for theological discussion we can then in chapters VIII–X expound our main thesis that an all-determinative questioning does not have the last word if we are to talk meaningfully about meaning.

III. MEANINGFUL?

WHAT does it mean to ask about meaning? This question brings us to a crossroads. On the one hand lies something that is totally given, unavoidable, set in a certain relation. This is the objective meaning. It is the content, the what, of all experience and action. On the other hand the question of meaning can be one of purpose, the why or to what end. The latter question is posed when something seems to be unintelligible, unrelated, without foundation. This is the question of meaning in the narrower sense. It seeks to justify what happens and the way it happens.

For the basic distinction there is biblical support that might help us. For all the historical distance it has not been outdated materially, for it contains an abiding question. We find it in Ecclesiastes, sometimes called the Preacher, as in the German Bible. The author was a wisdom teacher in Israel usually dated in the postexilic period (perhaps in the mid-3rd century B.C.). Wisdom teachers were trying to understand the order of things and the course of events so as to plan life and make it responsible. But in the course of his investigation this teacher came up against the limits of what we can know. One of these limits was the way that times are set for what we experience and do. These times fix boundaries within which we move and alone can move:

> For everything there is a season, and a time for every matter under heaven:

a time to be born, and a time to die;

a time to plant, and a time to pluck up what is planted;

a time to kill, and time to heal;

a time to break down, and a time to build up;

a time to weep, and a time to laugh;

a time to mourn, and a time to dance;

a time to throw away stones, and a time to gather stones together;

a time to embrace, and a time to refrain from embracing;

a time to seek, and a time to lose;

a time to keep, and a time to throw away;

a time to tear, and a time to sew;

a time to keep silence, and a time to speak;

a time to love, and a time to hate;

a time for war, and a time for peace.

With these antitheses the author embraces human life from its beginning with entry into the world to its end with death. He is not merely looking, then, at the possibilities of decision on which action depends. Nor is he saying that all events are determined in such a way that we can accept them only as fate. To be sure we cannot decide on birth or death. Again, the seasons decide on when we should plant and weed. For residents in small states that are the football of the great powers, outbreaks of war or peace might be felt to be ineluctable blows of fate (or political events of a higher order that average people can no more influence than cosmic catastrophes). But much else, much that goes on in everyday life, is open to human choice and is decided that way. In board games (perhaps the point of casting and gathering stones)[1] everything may hang on the right move at the right time, but the players need not feel that they are puppets of fate. Each move, however, alters the situation and it cannot be recalled. Traders, too, for example, may only buy or sell at one time, they may keep in their account or not, and they must accept the risk of decision.[2] The same applies to staying silent or speaking, crying or laughing. There is such a thing as an eloquent

---

1. Cf. E. Pfleiderer, *Die Philosophie des Heraklit von Ephesus* (Berlin, 1886), 274f., discussed by K. Galling, "Das Rätsel der Zeit im Urteil des Kohelets (Koh. 3:1-15)," *Zeitschrift für Theologie und Kirche* 58 (1961), 10.

2. Galling, "Rätsel," 12.

silence, but in a conversation the listener cannot also speak. Nor can we laugh with eyes that are crying or cry with eyes that are laughing, even though profound sorrow and supreme joy do not exclude one another. Those who laugh cannot cry at the same time, so that our ability to laugh when crying is not a matter of conscious will or deliberate decision. We can do one or the other, but only one at one time. The same is true of killing and healing, and especially so when a physician wants to heal but does something that brings death because he does not do it at the right time for healing. Finally we have love and hate. The issue here is not that of moral values between which we need not choose because we have to be convinced that there is never a time for hate. That is not the issue here. The point is that when we love we cannot also hate (except in the case of psychological confusion). Real hate rules out love, but both are part of life, for love would not be what it is if there were no hate.

Our world, the world of our experience and action, contains these opposites that exclude one another. In every action and experience the opposite that constitutes its meaning is unavoidably excluded. At that moment, then, our reality is decided. By the exclusion of that which is indeed possible but which the reality of its opposite makes impossible, everything active, and when we look at birth and death everything passive, is decided. Life involves this kind of decision. Decision does not come merely with reflection about it or with the impression that the world is full of possibilities between which we may choose. Every matter or process has its time, and we see what it is the moment no time is left for its opposite. In this way we see not only that what is decided is in time and that only thus is it real, but also that the opposite can be possible. It remains possible in a nexus that contains what is actually done and experienced and its opposite, thus permitting repetition or on another occasion a different experience or decision. This rule gives meaning in the sense of content to every experience or action. It allows us to say what happens, no less and no more.

Whether we find what we do or what happens to us to be right, that is, at the right time, the favorable hour, is another question. It is the question whether we can see that what occurs is meaningful or whether we fail to find meaning in that which takes place irrevocably in time and finds fulfillment in it. Only to a certain extent is this question one of human freedom. We are free to the degree that our experience and action are meaningfully decided in the sense of content. There we always have room. Nevertheless, we cannot understand the structure of what happens in such a way as to build a plan of life on it. In all that we think may happen and we may try to do, thinking it is right, we cannot descry the future or find a basis for a solid calculating of life, that is, by successfully surveying not only the totality of our own existence but also reality in general in all its interlacings and causes and effects. For the attempt to achieve such a survey and in this way to decide what is the right time for doing this or that, Ecclesiastes gives no chance of success. This kind of undertaking is a violation of God's own working and God's assessment of creation: "I know that whatever God does endures forever; nothing can be added to it, nor anything taken from it; God has done this, so that all should stand in awe before him" (3:14). The real question of the right time, then, is whether in what we see to be given and in what we do ourselves we are in harmony with God's time in the context of his own working.

We thus leave the sphere of what we have thus far depicted as the space-time in which, in experience and action, we find meaning in the sense of content, that is, by the negation of possibilities that are not realized either because they do not happen or because we do not choose them. The question of the right time either of action or of experience that influences action advances a step to the point where we see the relations between all possibilities, and not just those that are actualized but all possibilities. Thus Ecclesiastes says: "I have seen the business that God has given to everyone to be busy with. He has made everything suitable for its time; moreover, he has put *olam* into their minds [or 'hearts'], yet they cannot find out what God has done from the beginning to the end" (3:10f.). Hebrew *olam* is usually translated "eternity," but I myself think the reference is to relation or connectedness. If so, what the passage is saying is that we have some sense of the interrelation of all things in their right time, namely, of their being determined in the context of God's own working. But this relation, that is, the congruence of what God determines and our action, we cannot assess or comprehend as regards either the details of the context or the whole (from the beginning to the end).

We are now at the crossroads in this question of meaning. It is obviously not enough to see specific experiences or actions as meaningful in the sense of content by noting that their opposites are in fact excluded.

We have also to inquire into the nexus of life into which all these experiences and actions are woven. At this point we come up against the limiting of our life by the right time that decides concerning what we experience and do. The determination on which the time of life's actualizing depends raises the question of the right time. This question stands related to time in general, not to the time that runs its course but to God's time, to fulfilled time, to what the Greek Bible calls *kairos*. The question relates to this determination, the place of the moment of time in the nexus of the time that God created and that he overrules. It is no longer enough to see that in specific actions and experiences the opposing possibility is excluded. It seems that we can remain aware of it against the background of what takes place and is done, and more that that, that we have to understand what takes place in terms of the fact that we know it to be set in a nexus that contains everything that is possible. Only thus do we seem to have the full world of the possible, and only in relation to it can we justify this or that actual experience or action. From this point onward we no longer need to say merely what happened (content); we have to understand why it happened (purpose).

Ecclesiastes, however, does not take this path. For him the question of the right time means unavoidable exertion with which we torture ourselves in vain. It force itself upon us but can easily lead us astray. By calling God's work the space-time in which we experience and act, Ecclesiastes is saying that God is the author of the world of possibilities. These possibilities are not indifferent, for in reality each one excludes the other. We are thus forced to raise the question if we are to decide aright and to accept aright that which is already decided.

Because God posits the right time for all things, we have to put the question of meaning. The rightness of the time, however, is for him and him alone to judge. With our questioning, then, we can never reach a conclusion. Everything we take to be well founded and use as a basis for our answer remains always provisional, transitory, futile. The real decision, the book tells us, is whether this unavoidable toil will lead to trust in God or whether it will be a reason for setting up our own context of meaning from which we exclude everything that is not meaningful. Those who accept God's work and thus enter into his time will not fall victim to the illusory and even senseless effort to stand above all the possibilities and to find out which of them make sense and which make no sense.

Ecclesiastes describes this false path without emotion. God has laid a "burden" (so RSV) on us, and "what gain have the workers from their toil?" (3:9f.). The burden is that of finding good purposes and goals and at the same time mastering the problem of acting at the right time. To ask about meaning is exhausting not merely because for all our hunting for the right time we may miss the proper moment for a specific act or experience. It is also and especially exhausting because we are trying to get above the interrelationship of things and their timing. Now, as the author realizes, this line of questioning is not fundamentally wrong, because God has given us in our hearts some inkling of the way things are connected. But no one can think out *(er-sinnen)* the nexus. We have to learn to live in it without trying to lay hold of it as a way of controlling our world. If we do the latter, the world will no longer be the reality of excluded possibilities. It will be a vacuum that is made to include all experience and action and it will be filled with problems arising out of the experiencing or not experiencing of what is meaningful. Meaning then becomes the final word that permits evaluation of existence as a whole. It will be my possible agreement with myself as agreement with the world.[3] It will be this in a way in which there can no longer be any distinction between God and the world.

When this consequence comes into view, Ecclesiastes calls a halt. With his question of the right time, of meaningful experience and action, the author wants to leave open the question of the goodness of God. He finds the gift of God in which we can rejoice and with which we can be satisfied in the simple fact that we live and are kept alive with all the joys that life bestows. "So I saw that there is nothing better than that all should enjoy their work, for that is their lot" (3:22).

The starting point here is the answer that is given, the fact that the time for things is set and we are creatures. The aim is to lead us to live in our time instead of burdening life with the riddle of time that is thus posed. It is not concealed that doubts and temptations remain, that we may even have the impression of being trapped in a hopeless and meaningless cycle (1:2-11). Paul would later recall this, but also lay claim in hopeful expectation to what Ecclesiastes bewails — the futility of the effort to get to the bottom of the course of things: "For the creation was subjected to futility, not of its own will but by the will of the one who

---

3. B. Welte, *Auf der Spur des Ewigen* (Freiburg im Breisgau, 1965).

subjected it, in hope" (Rom. 8:20). We have no reason to object if Ecclesiastes could not yet speak in this way. The warning that it gives us to accept the timing that is set and not to give way to yearning for unrealized possibilities is still valid. We catch an echo of it in Blaise Pascal when he complains that we are never satisfied with the present. We look ahead to the future as though it were coming too slowly and we would like to hasten its progress, or we recall the past and cling to it as though it had vanished too quickly. It is folly to roam about in times that are not ours and to forget the one that is, and futility to think about times that do not exist and to lose the only one that does because it is the present that usually offends us. We hide the present from ourselves because it troubles us, and if it treats us kindly we bewail seeing it vanish. We try to keep it as our future, and are bent on controlling things not in our power at a point in time at which we have no guarantee that we will even be alive. Those who examine their thoughts will all find that they are occupied with the past and the future. We hardly think about the present, and when we do it is only to kindle here a light that we will have at our disposal in the future. The present is never the goal. The past and the present are means; the future alone is the end. Hence we never live. We hope to live. It is unavoidable, then, that we are always preparing to be happy but never are.[4]

Due to this splintering the question of meaning arises in its absolute and life-threatening form. What Ecclesiastes has to say about the matter demands steps on a path from which deviation will always lead to error.

The message of Ecclesiastes calls for special notice here. We might derive from it instruction on the art of living: Take one day at a time just as it is; make the best of it; pluck it as ripe fruit (cf. the *carpe diem* of Horace); or at least get some taste of it even if you cannot savor it fully. Yet we might also see in Ecclesiastes a resigned acceptance of what the day brings because no one knows what will come tomorrow: "Let us eat and drink, for tomorrow we die," as Isaiah (22:13) has those say who do not perceive God's working. In fact, however, neither of these is the issue here. Ecclesiastes is insisting that we must not overlook or miss our lot even though we can never see the meaning of it. We can balk at our lot if we do not accept what is given us by God's creation and as God's creatures. What is appropriate for us is to live in time and

4. B. Pascal, *Pensées* (ET New York, 1958), 49f.

not to try to see everything from the beginning to the end. What is ours now, what happens to us now, is the divinely appointed meaning that we must not let go for the sake of some supposedly better fortune. What this meaning implies in detail, what it signifies, and how we can speak of it, such things the author leaves open, and they must be left open by us, too, at this point. It is enough for us to note that the author has made a distinction so that he may ask after meaning but not try to achieve it himself. He will arrive at meaning if he takes that which encounters him and that which he does and integrates them into the nexus that he views as meaningful.

The author distinguishes between the need for orientation that is rightly ours and the need for justification that crosses the boundaries of our humanity.[5] The first need is a very human one. It is posited by the time that all things have, including human life, and by our temporality of which we are aware when we focus on real things instead of simply dreaming about those that are possible. We need orientation because and to the extent that we have experiences and engage in actions that have meaning. "Meaning" in this regard means the direct determination of what we experience and do. It does not have the further sense to which orientation easily lets itself be led, that is, "meaning" as the totality of everything possible and real. What we experience and do is referred to something different, especially to the point in time at which it happens as God decides (says the author). Can we get beyond the fact of this determination? Do we not need perspectives from which to understand and accept and deal with what happens? Do we not have to go beyond the moment lest we achieve no more than complacent enjoyment of the moment?

The author does not deny that. But he plainly sees also a temptation. We may change the questions that are put to us by the determination of all things into our own questions about the meaning of life and the world. The need for justification then enters the dialogue. The constitutional need for orientation becomes the need to subject time in its course to ourselves and to give place to that within it which counts as meaningfully possible. In extreme cases the alternatives suggested by

5. For the distinction between the need of orientation and the need of justification cf. H. G. Ulrich, *Anthropologie und Ethik bei Friedrich Nietzsche . . .* , Beiträge zur evangelischen Theologie 68 (Munich, 1975), 83ff.

Ecclesiastes then call for rejection as unsettling possibilities that are a burden and a threat. They are possibilities that threaten our own existence and what seems to make life worth living. Some things in the list make sense: healing rather than killing, planting rather than plucking up, laughing rather than weeping, and certainly peace rather than war or living than dying. But if we disturb the ranking in that way we endanger the meaning of the whole, not the meaning of the world in and for itself, but the meaning for us who want to live and act meaningfully. Even if human individuals or cultures think more broadly and find a place for more possibilities in the knowledge that they are part of life, these possibilities, too, have their place and fix the meaning of existence. We are first asked: What is happening to me, and what can I, must I, should I do? But then the question put to us changes into the question about life itself: What meaningful experience and action does it have for me? This question pays heed to the world, but from the world we can hear only what it expresses in things. Absolute meaning, and not just the significance of this or that process or action, has to be brought out of the world of things and taken in hand. It must not be left in the concealment of the action of God that is beyond our human comprehension and our striving for self-certainty.

It is not that God does not allow us any fulfilled time. But this fullness is not to be measured by what we can basically make or represent. What we can justify when we ask about meaning can only make for us a nexus that throws us back on ourselves. In contrast to that kind of totality of meaning, Ecclesiastes sets the fulfilled time that consists of the coincidence of God's appointed moment and our right or timely action. In relation to the time that God has set for each thing, Ecclesiastes also asks about more than the mere facticity, about what happens and how it happens. But the book does not do more than ask. It does not move beyond perceptions of objective meaning. It does not presumptuously try to see the nexus of God's working. It realizes that that is impossible, and that to attempt it is to yield to temptation. It knows very well the difference between the meaningful and the meaningless. It knows how difficult is the question of the right time. But it goes no further with this than to express the difficulty of justifying life. If it did more, if it tried to search out the world's nexus of meaning, it would be led into self-justification.

It cannot achieve any such justification. It confesses this, and so it

turns to an awaiting of its lot, that is, the life that God gives in each of
its moments. It shows restraint in its inquiry into meaning. It is content
to perceive objective meaning without simply dragging in everything
that happens. In every determination of life's moments it perceives
God's working. In that context all things have their time even though
we may miss their right time. In confidence that all that takes place
under the sun (1:13) comes from God even though the link is hidden
from us, the author, even though somewhat skeptical, also finds joy in
life. And the determining of a time for all that happens does not suppress
the question of the right time but keeps it alive, for as God's determination it is also the opportunity that God grants us for our own experience and action.

IV. ACTION AND MEANING

PARAPHRASING Ecclesiastes 3:1-15 has shed light on the different ways in which things are meaningful that I have tried to explore more fully because to all appearances they are not widely studied. In the foreground is the meaning of action, in which case objective meaning frequently and without being noticed merges into the question of what is meaningful and of the meaning of action in a more general sense. It is to some extent understandable that what claims our attention primarily is not just the actual significance of what we experience and suffer but the meaning of action. In the case of action we can see more clearly that the why and wherefore is not always obvious. The same question arises as regards experience and suffering but usually only when a crisis of action and its possibilities is felt. To what end am I in the world, and why does the world exist at all? This is what we ask when the goal of life that we have set for ourselves has faded into the unattainable distance or when we have sought that which sustains our existence in things or people that have perished. The threads that hold life together have snapped. The question of the meaning of life arises because our action as a whole no longer achieves its goal.

This link between the meaning of existence and action is in vogue today, but it restricts the area of perception that for Ecclesiastes brings together experience, suffering, and action. The epitaph of Martinus von

1. F. von Lipperheide, *Spruchwörterbuch,* 4th ed. (Berlin, 1962), 238.

Bibrach at Heilbronn (died 1498)[1] also refers to the actual meaning of existence, not the question of its meaning, when it states:

I live, and know not how long,
I die, and know not when,
I go, and know not whither,
I am surprised I am so cheerful.

This surprise is related to that of the author of Ecclesiastes vis-à-vis the unexpected goodness of existence. He leaves the justification of his life to God because he sees himself set within the boundaries of time.

But this confidence that is won within such limits, hard by the skeptical observation of the signification of what we experience and do, cannot be forced. It can be hindered, however, if only action counts. If only possibilities of action count when we consider what has meaning or is meaningful or meaningless, then existence itself becomes a task, life becomes a special form of achievement, and reality becomes something we have to effect in part and control in part.

When and for what reason is the question of meaning reduced to that of the meaning of action? There is much to support the view that this is a modern idea, that in our own age reality has come to be seen as something we have to effect and its perception as a task. In a world that is only a world of work, even in all things that we can and do seize and grasp, perception is an activity and meaning has to be brought forth even though it is already there in things.

Old Testament wisdom, and the Greeks, too, saw it differently. For Plato and Aristotle meaning was fundamentally perception *(aisthēsis)* even in speech. Aristotle in particular devoted himself to an analysis of the meaning *(logos)* of linguistic expression.[2] Yet the meaning of action also has a special place for him, though not in the same sense as for us, for the question of meaning is not so dominant for him and his concept of action is more specialized and nuanced. In his *Nicomachean Ethics* he distinguished selection *(prohairesis)*, which judges and decides, action *(praxis)*, practical ability *(technē)*, and method *(methodos)*, the scientific

2. On this cf. W. Wieland, *Die aristotelische Physik: Untersuchung über die Grundlegung der Naturwissenschaft und die sprachlichen Bedingungen der Prinzipienforschung bei Aristoteles* (Göttingen, 1962), esp. 161 and 194.

following of a course. He could call all these "actions."[3] Each has a goal
(telos). There are different goals and goals of different rank, but common
to all actions is that they have their goal and are intelligible in terms of
it.[4] Each action, then, has meaning. It may not always be linked to
specific goals from which it may be expressly distinguished. It may have
its meaning in itself because it simply has to take place as it does. There
may be different degrees of success, as Aristotle shows by the example
of zither players, in which case we have playing and virtuoso or very
good playing.[5] But this example does not mean that there is no more
to human life than art. What Aristotle wants to show is that all action
is an expression of life and that it thus has objective meaning because
in it the active force of the soul *(energeia psychēs)* expresses itself in
conformity to the *logos*.[6] We might use "meaning" for *logos* here, "meaning" in the sense of the meaningful constitution of the world to which
we are referred in all our actions. By the *logos* we and the world are in
harmony. We are so in such a way that human action always has the
specific sense to which it is oriented.

To expound the fact that work has meaning in a meaningful reality,
Aristotle lists many activities that he calls expressions of vital living, for
example, trades, economics, politics, science, arts of many kinds, physical and intellectual training. This is all true of human beings, of those
who in addition to the physical existence and sense impressions that
they have in common with other creatures have the *logos* and by means
of it share in the goodness of the world. We express this relation by what
we do. Action, then, is not just living; it rests on understanding. We can
judge or measure what is or is not in accordance with what we intend
or not. Hence all human activity, whatever its social validity, aims at
what it must achieve in a harmony of its doer and the world. It is
oriented to the good that lies behind all action and that can never be
destroyed but can be established. This good has to be achieved, and that
depends on action in its various forms. Every act oriented to the good
has meaning, then, even though the multiplicity of human society

---

3. Aristotle *Nicomachean Ethics* 1.1, 1094a, 1f.; and 1.5, 1097a, 16ff.

4. Ibid. The goal toward which everything strives is *agathon* as both possession and
the good; cf. Plato *Gorgias* 499c.

5. Aristotle *Nicomachean Ethics* 1.6, 1098a, 11f.

6. Ibid., 1.6, 1098a, 7.

means that there are necessarily many different activities. Aristotle has
a concern both for the wealth of goods in life that demand meaningful
action and just as much, or perhaps even more, for the fact that all
actions are equal as regards their meaning. He certainly allows for very
different degrees of happiness that we feel when we successfully reach
a goal. He also takes into account that making music gives more satisfaction than enterprises that seek to do something specific, let alone
those that are no more than a means to an end. Finally there are rankings
in social worth. But these do not decide whether an act has meaning.
Even very elementary acts with no particular social status have meaning.
To take an example, though this is not Aristotle's, when I sit on a seat,
that is an act that has meaning. Only closer analysis shows how many
elements (presuppositions, expectations, etc.) there are in this act. An
act of this kind is self-evident; it is understood in terms of its own
happening. With no claim to special importance, it makes sense and it
is thus intelligent, as Aristotle would say.

In Aristotle the question of meaning stays within the limits of
objective meaning. He seeks the goal and orientation of acts and finds
in *logos* the vital element in human activity. *Logos* is the intelligent reason
that draws attention to the goodness of existence and enables us to see
the meaning of action. This does not mean that action always has value.
With that distinction ethics enters in. Ethics inquires into the good and
differentiates what has value from what has not. It considers what we
may undertake to reach a goal (we catch an echo here of the question
of the meaningful and the meaningless). Will this approach be reward-
ing? What is its value relative to the goal? All these questions have to do
with the scale of goods and do not take us beyond the meaning of action
even when it is a matter of the supreme good. Degrees of value are
certainly important ethically, but they are not decisive for life itself, for
we grasp them only within the given world. If a German translator finds
it necessary to use the expression *Sinn des Lebens* ("meaning of life"),
there is no basis for this in Aristotle's text, which simply uses "life" (in
the sense of spending it) even when it is a matter of the highest and
purest of goals of action.[7] The meaning of life is not a theme in an
ethics that induces evaluation of action in accordance with its goals.
Aristotle again would not by a long way have said that the meaning of

7. Ibid., 1.10, 1100b, 16.

life is action, and the converse would have been quite unthinkable for him. His starting point is that life and action, at least from an ethical angle, are one. Only thus can he focus on the what, the intention, of individual acts. Meaning as an answer to the question "Why do I live at all?" did not come within his range of vision. His thinking lay too closely within the polis and the cosmos for him to raise so basic and comprehensive a question.

Nevertheless, in retrospect at least, we do find here approaches to an expansion of the question of meaning. Aristotle linked the question of meaning to ethics, which he worked up into a grandiose survey of the goodness of life in its many forms. In the further history of Western thought the good that formed for Aristotle the meaningful structure of the world of life, and of actions within it, came to be equated with meaning itself.[8] Values became steps of being that we have to climb in order to attain to life's fulfillment. Thus perception of the meaning of actions became subordinate to its discovery in the case of each action, it would now seem. But discovery then came to entail not merely finding but producing. It is then only a further step in the same direction for action as a whole to have the meaning of constructing the world and sustaining reality. The result is the question of meaning that eliminates different views of meaningful.

To examine this momentous transition more closely we must again look at the objective meaning of actions, at the sense that was the only one for Aristotle. Meaning in this sense adds nothing to an action, as we have seen, but makes it understandable in terms of the relevant relations. This is true even when an act does not have only one goal but has some other goal beyond the immediate one. For example, G. D. Kaufman, following L. Wittgenstein, refers to the complexity of a not easily identifiable action when watching a woodcutter and considering what was the ultimate *telos* of what he was doing. In felling a tree he might be using it for firewood but he might also plan to build a house or have some even better purpose.[9] His action does not at once disclose his intention. Even though it is obvious what he is doing, what he will

8. H. Kuhn, *Das Sein und das Gute* (Munich, 1962), esp. 275ff.; on Plato's influence, 201ff. Cf. also W. Weier's *Sinn und Teilhabe* for this tradition.

9. G. D. Kaufman, *Systematic Theology: A Historicist Perspective* (New York, 1968), 260f.

finally achieve is not yet evident. The meaning of his action relates to both purposes and perhaps to even more than the first two. Yet this has nothing whatever to do with the question whether his action is meaningful. If his action seems to be meaningless, it is only because its complexity hampers its ability to communicate. To stay with the same example, Boniface chopped down a tree in order to unmask a god as an idol. What he did made sense to those who watched him in the very extravagance of his purpose, which was totally outside the framework of the religion he encountered. It would be idle, however, to speculate on what might have happened if someone had destroyed the altar that Boniface set up. What would be in the one case the twilight of the gods would be the refuting of the faith in the other. Today no one would suspect sacrilege when a tree is felled. People would not understand such an action as a missionary message either.

Sociology has introduced observations of the same kind. It is sociology and not philosophy or philosophical ethics that now seeks primarily to describe actions in terms of the question of their meaning. Sociology does not concern itself in the first instance with their objective meaning, for in the history of humanity and the shifts in cultures and societies this is not always evident any more. Too many things are beyond our understanding and have even ceased to make any sense. What has happened, is happening, and will happen does not always speak adequately for itself. It needs some further interpretation to make itself plain. Sociology tries to discharge this hermeneutical task by bringing to light the social and cultural context in which an action has its terms of reference and can thus be understood. The context may be artificially restored by reconstruction. This, too, is a finding of meaning within a given framework as it were, that is, the finding of meaning in such a way that what is done is intelligible against the background of the purpose. The hermeneutical possibilities in this regard even cover processes of questionable meaningfulness. Such a situation arises when the social context of an action is lost or changed. Even then it is possible in retrospect to understand the action, even to give it meaningful life again, which means to give it (again) a meaning if this is its *own* original meaning.

This is the point of the "interpretive (or 'understanding') sociology" that the works of Max Weber pioneered.[10] Weber described this as a

10. M. Weber, "Über einige Kategorien der verstehenden Soziologie" (1913) in

science that interprets and understands social action and in this way tries to show the causes behind its course and effects. Action means human conduct (whether outward or inward, whether in the form of action, refraining from action, or experiencing) insofar as the person or persons who act relate some subjective meaning to it. Social action, however, is that which in accordance with the meaning intended by the person or persons acting relates to the conduct of others and is oriented to this as it takes its course.[11]

In this definition "meaning" has to do with the fulfilling of an intention. Only action of this kind can be regarded as intelligent and intelligible. As regards the question of meaning, then, much of what we have had in view thus far is left out of account. Linking meaning to actions also, almost imperceptibly, entails a new evaluation of meaning in general. Weber thinks that the course of human action, or human expression of any kind, is open to meaningful interpretation.[12] This thesis sounds self-evident, but it is not. Meaning here is no longer, or no longer exclusively, the reference of an action to something that makes it intelligible. Meaning gives place to interpretation. As meaning is linked to interpretation it becomes dependent on what may sometimes be a newly created framework of validation that allows us to distinguish between the meaningful and the meaningless, between an action that is full of meaning and one that simply takes place to no purpose.

This is the decisive change. We are no longer establishing objective meaning but asking after a meaning that alone can be regarded as meaningful in the true sense. "Meaningful" is now set in a framework of explanation that shows how meaning arises. But the explaining itself wants to be regarded as an activity that shows itself to be meaningful. It is the giving or establishing of meaning, and it is so precisely where no objective meaning is immediately to be found.

We are now moving on a theoretical level, though this does not have to mean that it has no practical significance. On the contrary! The

Gesammelte Aufsätze zur Wissenschaftslehre, ed. J. Winckelmann, 4th ed. (Tübingen, 1973), 427ff. For a development of Weber's approach cf. A. Schütz, *The Phenomenology of the Social World* (ET Chicago, 1967).

11. Weber, "Soziologische Grundbegriffe" (1921), in *Gesammelte Aufsätze*, 482.

12. Weber, *Roscher and Knies: The Logical Problems of Historical Economics* (ET London, 1975), 65.

turning of the question of meaning into a discovering, giving, and establishing of meaning helps to overcome a crisis that to all appearances is caused by the fact that on a broad front action seems to bear no relation to anything. Whether this is actually the case or an exaggerated need for explanation lies behind it, we can only guess and not decide within the limits of our present study. From sociological models of explanation, however, we may conclude that meaning can be sought for different if inwardly related reasons. Action seems to have no objective meaning when we see in it no point of reference by which to understand it either outwardly or inwardly, when it seems to be arbitrary and to tell us nothing specific. Again, action is found to be meaningless when it can be related to no goal or purpose that we can recognize in a given social context, when it falls outside the context. The result is finally the same when we cannot distinguish any specific objective meaning, when it makes no difference with what line of conduct we arouse the attention of others. Arbitrary action might indeed have some objective meaning, but it is hard to identify this in terms of the goal, and it is thus in danger of becoming meaningless because it leads nowhere or may be interchanged with some other action.

This decay in the assignment of objective meaning to action goes hand in hand with the development of sociology as a science, though whether as cause or effect we need not discuss here. The decay is everywhere apparent and attracts the attention of analysts and therapists alike. Those who do not describe individual actions in their objective meaning but ask in addition whether they are meaningful correspond to a mood of the age in which showing that an action is meaningful plays an important social role.

The hermeneutical task of explaining actions as meaningful has thus become a comprehensive one of clarification. Basic actions must be followed in their development and their intentions brought to light. A sociology that proceeds in this way is no longer content to do no more than describe what happens. It must explain why it happens and how. This is the most far-reaching step thus far into the question of meaning. We have to understand how the reality that presents itself to us has arisen. We no longer see it completely if we look at it simply as Aristotle did, or in his own way the author of Ecclesiastes. The latter would have asked how reality came into being and therefore how it is constituted. Aristotle would have tried to show how it is constructed. Sociologists who seek to bring meaning to light also want information on the structure of the world but in such a way that they can follow it constructively and thus at the same time cause the world to come into being afresh. The extent of the world is not yet fixed definitively. We humans constantly have to grasp it in its full range and take it in hand in all its breadth and depth. The process in which society fashions its own world establishes meaning and makes it known. This character of actions sheds light on the ranking that is allotted to action as regards world development. Action has meaning because — and insofar as — reality is created by the establishment of meaning.

The question of meaning becomes an acute one for this reason. For the reconstruction of the world from the bottom up, not just in its historical course but above all in its present genesis, finds out what may be called meaningful and what seems to be meaningless because it has no importance and is hard to comprehend. Explanations of basic actions no longer view it as enough to show what things are included as meaningful in a nexus of authoritative interpretations within a culture, religion, or society, as distinct from many other things that were regarded as meaningful by other cultures and in other times. The nexus of meaning of the world as such is now the basis by which to say whether an action has to be called meaningful. The point is not that always and without exception reality depends on the human positing of meaning. The point is that what is meaningful decides what will emerge as significant and it is humans who have a normative part in this. Not given meaning but the giving of meaning is what counts.

As the advocate of this type of explanation, scientific work sets the pace in the finding and establishing of meaning. It prepares the setting that permits us to list processes as meaningful and that thereby gives direction to human action. We have touched on this tendency already, but we must come back to it because it keeps alive the question of meaning and wherever possible raises it.

Academic sociology offers an example. In this discipline Peter L. Berger among others writes that "the most important function of society is nomization. The anthropological presupposition for this is a human craving for meaning that appears to have the force of instinct. Men are congenitally compelled to impose a meaningful order upon reality."[13]

13. P. Berger, *The Sacred Canopy: Elements of a Sociological Theory of Religion* (New York, 1967), 22f.

This quotation shows that something more and different is now meant by "meaning" than what we meant earlier by "the meaning of action." The meaning of individual and social action that Berger has in view is intended to exclude what is meaningless in order to make possible the experience of a reality that will form the framework for everything that counts as meaningful. Weber with his "meaningful interpretation of actions" was still thinking of the activity of an understanding that expounds the course and effects of actions. Now, however, the establishing of meaning is declared to be a basic activity on which everything that can be called meaningful depends.

Similarly Niklas Luhmann calls meaning the basic concept of sociology.[14] Like Berger, he first sees in meaning a phenomenon that is always "constituted" and built up, and that can thus be disclosed as it is constituted. The constitution of meaning, however, means two things. First, meaning is the meaningful structure of phenomena, data, and actions by which we have access to them. Its constitution is then an act of upbuilding that takes place in our human encounter with the world and that comprehends or influences the structure. More precisely, meaning as the basis of all human life rests on the interaction of meaning as reality that is already constituted and meaning as reality that is still being constituted. Meaning expresses what is generally experienced as reality, from elementary processes, for example, the daily affairs with which we demonstrate our confidence in the world that sustains us, to the final human questions that can be answered only if reality is shown thereby to be bearable. Religion, too, cooperates in the constitution of reality in this way. This is its function for society and for the individuals living their lives within it.

These varied and often highly complex processes might all be summed up as a mastering of contingency, and this technical term describes one of the most fascinating but also the most attractive concepts in modern sociology.[15] What it signifies is that everything that is

14. See p. 17 n. 24; also N. Luhmann, *Funktion der Religion* (Frankfurt, 1977), 20ff.; and *Gesellschaftsstruktur und Semantik: Studien zur Wissenssoziologie der modernen Gesellschaft*, vol. I (Frankfurt, 1980), 17f.

15. H. Lübbe speaks of the practice of mastering contingency and in this way combines the explanations of Luhmann, A. Gehlen, T. Luckmann, and G. Dux in terms of the sociology of religion; cf. "Religion nach der Aufklärung," in *Religion als Problem der Aufklärung*, ed. T. Rendtorff (Göttingen, 1980), 174.

or that takes place must primarily be experienced as real. The world is never, as it were, complete. It is only partly there. It builds up itself (Luhmann would say as a system) every moment for each individual and for humanity as a whole. Only thus does it show itself to be the real world — never self-contained, always limited by what is real for humanity and those who share in the constituting of the world. In actuality reality is, of course, complete, yet it is always in a state of flux, for what we assert to be reality is at the same time a momentary adoption of that which is constituted and therefore accessible. We experience only that which manifests itself, so that only as it is, is it there for us, though it also might not be, or might be in some different way. It does not have to be, but it can, and it is thus contingent. Everything that is possible but not necessary is contingent.[16] If it is to be grasped and posited, it must first be made determinable. Thus our world arises, the nexus of all that emerged from the state of possibility to that of reality, the system that includes everything that is there for us but that also hints at further possibilities.[17]

Contingency has to be mastered. This thesis is often taken to mean (wrongly, I think) that one has to take accidental or surprising events in hand in order to make them tolerable. Along these lines the mastering of contingency would establish meaning in critical situations, for example, great turning points in life, birth and death, inconceivable sufferings, or overwhelming disasters. Things which come upon individuals or individual social groups or the race as a whole in a way that destroys the fabric of the world they know have then to be reintegrated by some special effort, and their meaning disclosed, if life is to go on. In a society in which there is division of labor, professionals in the establishing of meaning, versed in the mastering of contingency, will then be able to make life that has been disrupted understandable in terms of some higher vantage point, and in this way to build a bridge over the abyss that has opened up in the familiar world with the life-threatening break. Religious leaders will obviously be claimed and will come forth as those who can master contingency in this way. In the past this is what the religions were able to do, and it is what they still wish to do today.

Luhmann considers and even explains the concept along such lines,

16. Luhmann, *Funktion der Religion,* 187.
17. Ibid., 21f.

but for him the mastering or contingency is not restricted to the greater or lesser disruptions of daily life. We do not experience contingency only when individuals or societies are thrown off their usual course and have to work their way through a reality that they can no longer understand. Contingency is more often and much earlier mastered in all life and action. It is mastered precisely in what seems to be everyday and trivial, for example, sitting on a seat or saying something obvious or seeing something familiar. There are, of course, different forms and degrees of mastery; and final questions, for example, the questions of life and death, play a special role in this regard. Nevertheless, we are always engaged in mastering contingency. We are always seeking meaning even if silently by simply experiencing and acting. For all experiencing and acting has to be accompanied by some expression of the world. It needs meaning that will show what is real, and how we can deal with it, including a reference to all that is possible against the background of what is now reality.

Can there still be here a decisive distinction between objective and nonobjective meaning? Luhmann will accept such a distinction to the degree that the latter is the supporting context within which we may establish the former. The former is for him a "much more general phenomenon that is necessarily given with human experience and action." But he is disturbed by the expectation, expressed in the distinction, that we can take the latter sense in a "conceptually more univocal" way than the former. "The establishing of a meaningful context of life seems to be for sociologists a matter that is far richer in presuppositions, far more dependent on historically and culturally divergent premises, than it is for theologians." For this reason there are at work for him "variables in social structure at this point, and especially considerations regarding the form of differentiation in social systems. Dependent on these in detail is what may be experienced in any specific system as evident or plausible or obligatory. Hence a very obviously functional concept like the mastering of contingency, which shows the transition from objective to nonobjective meaning to be a selective process."[18]

We have here the decisive catchwords. It is by selecting from what is objectively meaningful in experience and action that we achieve a

---

18. Cf. Luhmann's response by letter (1.7.1980) to my address "Theologische Betrachtungen zur Sinnfrage," now in *Sinn und Wahrheit*.

meaningful context for life. Along these lines each individual society or partial social system within it does what the mastering of contingency implies. What we call the "world" is the result of a process of selection and limitation by which we exclude as meaningless that which has no sustaining significance for us. In this process norms, values, beliefs, and final answers to final questions play a part. These may also be described as selections insofar as they contribute to the constitution of the world what is of vital importance for the preservation of systems, for individuals, for social systems, and finally for the human world as a whole. This function is the standard by which sociology assesses what is meaningful. Involved is the interpretation that brings out the meaning or significance of actions, texts, and expressions of life of all kinds even when this meaning can only be disclosed or brought back to life again. This is the victory of sociology over life once life is made understandable as the strategy of mastering life.

At this point the question of meaning is unavoidable and omnipresent. What else should we ask about or take note of? The magic slogan "mastering of contingency" gives further luster to the question of meaning, which hermeneutics, the discipline of understanding, had already imposed on written texts in the nineteenth century. If hermeneutics was previously content to pronounce with some confidence on what a traditional text was saying (its meaning), it becomes a universal understanding of the world through speech. All the world becomes the text that is then interpreted along literary lines, and a reality of understanding results in which we become understandable for the first time to ourselves. As "interpretive (or 'understanding') sociology" and its successors explain each act in life as a meaningful action, the activity of interpretation becomes a principle of action. Even that which seems to be meaningless for an individual or a generation can be shown to be meaningful by interpretation, or at least made understandable; otherwise it would not even be there. Apart from meaning nothing can be.

We can only indicate here the theoretical implications of this almost ineluctable expansion of the question of meaning in order to draw attention to some of the by no means merely practical consequences. First we must look at the importance of action in this whole question. It is not that pure activity should be given the first and last word. On the contrary, Luhmann gives to experience, too, the function of mastering contingency. But it is a function, and achievement, of a special kind that is assigned to experience of reality. This is why the concept of mastering contingency is so attractive. It takes something that happens to individuals and humanity, that might at times overtake them, and describes it as an object that they must work on and work over. Even when we have to let something happen to us, when the time of active doing of things is at an end or interrupted, we are active in other ways. Even though we cannot effect anything, we can still be significant or signify something. Thus in a supremely sublime way the world becomes a total world of work in which all actions are transformed into modes of expression for the giving of meaning. In the process, however, the variety of action that Aristotle tried to describe is lost. Every action is now burdened with the demand to contribute in some way, and if need be in a very indirect way, to the meaning of the world. The meaning of this or that act alone is no longer the question, nor is the more immediate or more distant goal with which it is performed without any further claim. The meaning of action in general is now the question. And whereas Aristotle differentiated *praxis,* as meaningful action, from all other activities, in our thinking and vocabulary *praxis* has come to be interchangeable with *technē, methodos, prohairesis,* and all other activities, so that it has lost its special role.

In consequence no act can now be so self-evident that the question of its meaning is superfluous and might even destroy its inherent meaning. What kind of meaning does prayer have? The ostensibly practical people who ask this see no point in prayer as speaking to God and before him. They may indeed try to say what it is that we hope to attain or achieve by invoking God, that is, assistance as the changing of a critical situation or as the changing of our own attitude so that we can accept or understand what cannot be changed. But such things might be reached in other ways. Prayer as a function can be replaced. It might be thought of and used as a complaint, or as the expression of a demand, or as an accusation or a cry of distress, but surely not any longer as thanksgiving or praise to God. For those who offer thanksgiving and praise no longer want to add anything to what they say or to achieve anything or to make any further point. This means that prayer of this kind has no place for the question of meaning. For this question, raised comprehensively with a view to mastering contingency, changes all action into an effecting of something. Hence we have to ask what the action achieves, even if it be only the basic thing that is demanded of all of us, namely, that the world be built up and preserved.

The totality of meaning comes to light in the fact that nothing exists apart from it. In practice this means that all things and each thing can be interpreted, that is, that their meaning can be disclosed. Even the meaningless can be seen only in its reference to meaning. The meaningless can thus be brought into being only as meaning.[19] We see this in the story of the hare and the tortoise. Those who know how to handle meaning as a cosmic formula are already at the goal while others tire themselves out by endless chasing and questioning. But this superior position has its price. The presupposition that is claimed here is that meaning is always a social product, a common achievement of individuals and ultimately of society as a whole. Those who want to adjust to contingency — and we cannot live without doing so — have to reckon with others as well as themselves, difficult and risky though this might be in detail.[20] They have to enter into relations and keep these relations intact if meaning is to arise and remain as a context. Meaning thus involves communication, which means speech insofar as it comes to expression, but which also transcends speech; it is rooted in the mastering of contingency as action that creates meaning.

Here is the explanation why we can no longer talk of meaninglessness or nonsense within the framework of communication and therefore of society, which maintains itself by giving meaning. This framework, however, is not just the social background and network of references that is always implied in the exposition of actions and that is conditioned by many historical circumstances and social processes but that for this reason remains unchangeable and has to be understood

19. Luhmann, *Funktion der Religion,* 21; and cf. M. Heidegger, *Being and Time,* where he argues that we can never set meaning and being in antithesis to what is coming to be or to being as the sustaining ground of what is coming to be, since this ground is accessible only as meaning even if it be the abyss of meaninglessness.

20. Luhmann, "Sinn als Grundbegriff der Soziologie," in Habermas and Luhmann, *Theorie der Gesellschaft oder Sozialtechnologie — Was leistet die Systemforschung?* (Frankfurt, 1971), 62f., where he makes the point that all experience and all action relating to another is doubly contingent in the sense that it depends on the other as well as myself, and I must see the other as an alter ego who is just as free and capricious as I am. My expectations of the other are met only as both of us set up the presuppositions for this and this condition is taken into account and also expected.

thus. Sociology started with this observation, and along these lines it could and can make itself understandable. But now it has to be shown how the world is constituted as a whole in which society participates. This is the situation at the end of the modern period, when, it is worth noting, sociology is looking beyond specific and limited social groups to "society," or making it plain that such social groups are only partial systems within this society. This means, however, that no longer can any semantic distinction be made between objective and nonobjective meaning. That which can show the imaginary total "society" to be objectively meaningful must also be nonobjectively meaningful, since anything else has already been ruled out. If anything cannot be made intelligible under the rubric of this society it cannot be finally described or properly perceived.

But is it not this precisely that triggers the crisis of orientation that the question of meaning entails? This crisis arises once a society that we can scrutinize no longer achieves what is demanded of it. Any deviation from society, no matter how it may be caused, is a threat to meaning. And if the way out of the crisis is the construction of alternative systems of meaning or totalities of meaning, the problem is compounded, and the only solution is to engage in increasingly comprehensive formal construction.

Social theory as we have sketched it offers a remarkably ambivalent picture when it takes up the question of meaning along such lines. Because it has nothing to say outside of meaning, it explains away the crisis of meaning of which so many speak. For Luhmann nothing, strictly, can be devoid of meaning or remote from it, so that there is no ground for complaint.[21] In any case, if there is reason to complain, it is due to failures in organization in the mastering of contingency. But more and more parts of society refuse to let themselves be listed among those who are deficient in that way. The impression of a crisis of meaning that has flooded broad sectors of our civilization for over a decade did not arise merely with the decay of established values but came to expression as a crisis of the action that has to do directly with reality and that is supposed to offer a context of life for each individual. If this action of society is renounced, then success becomes rarer in appropriating one's own meaning and achieving harmony with it. Strategies of

21. Luhmann, *Funktion der Religion*, 20.

establishing meaning cause alienation. They locate meaning in anonymous organizations (technology, bureaucracy, science) that view themselves no longer as contingent but as necessary.

The protest against them that erupted in the mid-1960s did not at
first inscribe the question of meaning on its banners. It proposed alternative action that in opposition to meaningless work and the mere
functioning of people and machines would give a new meaning, the
meaning of humanity. Trust in the power of praxis to create meaning
was still alive here, but the praxis was now different, born out of opposition to the empty course of a controlled world. But the expectations
aroused by the new praxis proved deceptive, either because they could
not permeate or change everyday activity, or because the sense of getting
very close to reality by actions had to be constantly renewed and constantly wore out again, or finally because the community experience
that was generated by common foes did not prove to be supportable in
the long run. There thus came a swing back to the question of meaning.
Many discovered an inner dimension that goal-oriented action did not
touch, and by means of elementary experiences in building community
they sought even in irrational forms of experience or a disconnecting
of consciousness the direct contact that praxis for all its promises had
failed to give. Both shifts in the search for meaning — the onward-
thrusting euphoria of praxis and the reversal of this into inner self-
experience — had the same root, namely, dissatisfaction with social reality and its claim to be a medium for reality.

In the musical *Hair* a young American from the Midwest, shortly
before his call up to Vietnam, is in a New York passage in which the
crowds hurry past him, and he asks:

Where do I go?
Follow my heartbeats?
Where do I go?
Follow my hands?
Where do they lead me
and will I ever discover
why I live and die?
Why do I live?
Why do I die?
Where do I go?

Tell me why
Tell me where
Tell me why
Tell me where
Tell me why.[22]

Although it has a different ring, this is a counterpart to the epitaph of
Magister Martinus. Martinus, however, could be astonished at his joy,
which is denied to our contemporaries.

We seem to have here not only a different language but a different
world from that of the sociological finding of meaning. But the question:
What meaning is there in this? is the reverse side of the fact that we
instinctively ask after meaning in order not to be wandering about
disoriented in chaos. Precisely in a perfectly organized metropolis this
chaos can cry out for meaning. If meaning can come from the giving
of meaning in which we must each have a part, then this meaning
escapes those who are actually or symbolically out of work. People who
cannot explain themselves in their world, reading themselves into it and
then seeing themselves in terms of it, find themselves shut out and they
ask why they exist at all. The need for orientation that makes us ask
after meaning becomes extremely radical here because it is inquiring
into the basis of things, and it is doing so in such a way that this basis
is explained as an act of giving meaning. The more this establishing of
meaning is seen as a process of working out the meaning, and the more
society is made responsible for it, the more keenly is the loss of meaning
felt when the forms of social organization that arise bypass individuals
or even stand opposed to them. The fact that meaning is no longer
visible can thus be a consequence of the fact that it was formerly expected as something that would be created.

We have now approached from another angle the crucial point in
the question of meaning in its absolute, all-embracing, omnipresent
sense as inquiry into meaning as a sustaining basis for life, the world,
and history. We have seen things now from the standpoint of the apparent contradiction between a crisis of meaning that has become a
cultural phenomenon and a theory of society that uses explicit mean-

22. Sauter uses the translation *Woh geh ich hin,* but has the English in the note. —
TRANS.

inglessness and even nonsense simply as an opportunity to transform it into meaning as a form of social experience and action. Those who ask about the why and the whither are constantly making the affirmation that they themselves are creatures that understand meaning. Worldwide complaints about meaningless work and existence that has no meaning provide an occasion to seek new forms of establishing meaning. Religious natures find fertile soil for their plants here. They suddenly meet with applause for their previously ignored protest against a nexus of life that has become mechanical, against a rationalized world. They do not note that they have themselves for a long time been caught in interpretations of meaning that simply promote another form of mastering contingency, perhaps to an inordinate degree.

The question of meaning encounters us today in two forms: first, in the void as a failure to understand, as moving along a path that has no goal, as a fatalistic abandonment of the distinction between meaningful moments in life and a life that is meaningful in the sense of value; second, as a diligent establishing of meaning that seizes and shapes everything, as a fanatical readiness to posit meaning necessarily because it can never be given up, because it is our task to assert it. For both fatalists and fanatics the world as it is has no meaning. At this point the question of meaning shows its two faces, which are nevertheless closely related.

Common to both is the linking of meaning to integration and ordering. If we are "congenitally impelled to impose a meaningful order upon reality" (Berger), then the world seems to us to be indeterminate, disorderly, and even chaotic so long as it eludes the grasp of active understanding. Everything is originally without meaning. Only on this premise can the factor of meaning become the thread that helps us in part to weave the web of the world. The question of the whither, whence, wherein, and why participates in the premise inasmuch as it seeks to locate the whole origin and future within the limits of a world in which all things are related to one another and only in this way can make sense. The limits here may be very broad. They may embrace heaven and earth, God and humanity, history from beginning to end. But only within these points of reference, this context that is without gaps though unpredictable, can reality be grasped from the very roots and taken in hand.

The sociological explanation tries to make the world understandable in its development as a historical evolution, as the self-unfolding of society. In the process it is inspired by a concern that any objective or nonobjective meaning which other interpretations might have proposed should be forgotten so that important elements of reality that are not social have no place and will sooner or later wither away. Meaning is sought not least because the world threatens to become smaller but also seems to be increasingly complex and unpredictable, and therefore valuable possibilities are missed. Humanity pushes out of its memory, which depicts the world,[23] things that it has to recall and view as contingent. Sociologists seek to counteract this forgetfulness by again laying stress on meaning once the process of establishing meaning, even if only traces of it are present, has been completed in a way that leaves no gaps. Sociology that works on meaning and invests with meaning makes an inventory of social life and commends itself to society as a kind of memory aid.

The need for such a function is undoubtedly growing. The only question is whether this global bookkeeper that seeks to store up all events and their backgrounds as "meaning" is not itself forgetting the decisive thing, and indeed inevitably overlooking it, namely, the world as *creation*. It is not that the concept of creation escapes sociological cataloguing. Parts of the theological tradition are quoted in sociological explanations, and investigations like those of Berger and Luhmann can have at times the form of surveys of the history of religion that put many of the programs of modern theology on the track of intellectual links. But when Luhmann recalls what theologians say about God the Creator, with the help of a reference to the contingency formula, he seeks to show how everything can be explained but no real distinction any longer made. If we trace the whole world back to God, the world itself has nothing to say. This may have implications for adjustment to the forms of social life and their description from this angle, but it does not allow any mastering of contingency except by reference back to a first cause that determines everything. God, then, is no more than the utmost conceivable unity that in itself erases all distinctions, such as that of good and evil or the old and the new.[24]

23. Luhmann, "Sinn als Grundbegriff," 49f.

24. Luhmann, *Funktion der Religion*, 130, 188, 204f. We cannot explain God solely in terms of the concept of contingency (208).

That much theology today thinks and speaks along such lines is incontestable, but we may question whether it ought to speak in this way. We can put this question, of course, only if we leave the framework of establishing and understanding meaning and agree that it is thus hard to show what the question really is. If not, we can hardly avoid the suspicion that we will be back to meaning by a different route. For — we recall — without meaning nothing exists, or at least nothing intelligible can be said. At this point, however, we must ask in a more rudimentary form than previously: What is the issue, *meaning or truth?* I deliberately raise this question directly at this juncture without preparing the ground for it. The criterion of meaning certainly does not allow any thoughts that are not already related to meaning and that can always be formulated as meaning. Nevertheless, truth cannot be viewed on the same level as meaning.

The creation story tells us pictorially that God fashioned the world out of the formless waste and void. He did so by separating light and darkness, heaven and earth, land and water, various kinds of living things, and human beings and the rest of the integrated world. Then of all that he created, both as a whole and in detail, he said that it was very good (Gen. 1:31). Creation depends on this assessment; it can endure only so long as it is pronounced. The "very good" is not a quality that the Creator ascribes to himself. Nor does it simply mean that we have here a perfect project that is still to be executed. The "very good" stands over creation, the finished world, because the goodness of God is really present in it, in the arrangement that gives to every creature the living space it needs. The world exists in virtue of the other order that God has laid down and that later, when human beings have violated it and the flood has overwhelmed all things, he will expressly confirm as the covenant of creation (9:9-17). But already at the beginning, as the biblical author depicts it, human beings forsook their position in creation. It was not enough for them to live their lives and to dress and keep the garden entrusted to them (2:15). They snatched after the forbidden fruit that promised them knowledge of what is good and evil (3:5). Eating this fruit would put them above good and evil, not beyond it, but above it in the sense that they could decide between the two on the basis of an all-comprehensive view ("good and evil" not being objects of practical reason but denoting the whole). This very step outside the divine prohibition, the attractive opportunity to view the whole and to make autonomous decisions on basic matters within this view, becomes the fatal perversion which simply shows those who are supposedly in the divine image that they have lost their dignity and must hide. They have not kept the Creator's command and prohibition but tried to form their own opinion regarding it. They wanted to get to the bottom of it but would have perished in the process had not God kept them alive.

In place of an explanation of the world and its application to the inner division of the world into good and evil, the biblical story of creation and the fall puts the verdict and command of God: the verdict that differentiates the truth of creation from the falsity of human life, the command that directs human beings to life in the truth. We cannot put to the verdict and command of God the question of their meaning without losing our creaturehood and our place in creation. We cannot trace them back to something that lies behind them and that we can grasp in such a way as to be able to pass our own verdict and give ourselves a command and prohibition based on our own insight. We cannot derive the verdict and command of God from anything because they are the beginning of all human perception. Certainly we can and must expound them to the degree that the question of their meaning, that is, what they say and how they affect us and our perception, is appropriate. But they are not subject to the question of meaning in the sense that they may be set forth as a giving of meaning and creatively imitated by us as such. Only when we observe this boundary that is set to the question of meaning, only when God's verdict and command stand between the right question and our own question that seeks orientation, is what we say about God protected against the making of God into a contingency formula which first promises to master all things and ends up not knowing how to say anything that has any power of differentiation, the result being that in the long run the term *God* is indefinable and can just as well be replaced by other terms.

The sociological explanation instead puts the world in an unceasing process in which there have to be ever and again new acts that constitute it as a dwelling place for society. From this standpoint of historical development the biblical creation story seems to be an ancient way of describing what we have to do — something that in substance may be more precisely described in other ways. The order that the biblical story saw as posited once and for all has to be constantly set up in order to preserve the world from the chaos that always surrounds it. In other words, indeterminate contingency, that is, anonymous chance and dumb facticity, has to be transformed into determinable contingency in order that it may be mastered.[25] But did not the Bible mean the same thing when it said that God made the basic antitheses light and darkness and later good and evil, salvation and perdition? It is tempting to extend the thought of this order, to picture creation as an ongoing process in which God has set the world before us as an ensemble of possibilities at our disposal that can complete the work with the help of the antitheses that we must imitate in our own orders and arrangements if the world is to be comprehensible.

The conclusion of the biblical story, however, blocks the path from the history of creation to later history with the verdict that God pronounces on his work and the associated beginning of God's rest on the seventh day (Gen. 2:2f.). With this general pause in creation God does not abandon his world or leave it to the course of history. Even less does he let it become a self-resting cosmos. God puts creation under the promise of his presence. It is secure in his faithfulness. At the same time, he sets limits for creation against itself by defining it as his own good and finished work.

The rest of God rather than his creative work sheds a normative light on all human work. This work of ours has the sabbath command as its boundary. As God rested from all his work, so we in his covenant should interrupt our work one day in the week and think of his finished creation (Exod. 20:8-11; the other version of the commandment in Deut. 5:12-13 recalls the freeing of Israel from enforced labor in Egypt, i.e., from subjection to restless activity that is not in keeping with our calling and leaves no room for praise of God). A story from the days of wilderness wandering (Exod. 16:11-30) elucidates the commandment. The grumbling people, who look back with longing on the fleshspots of Egypt, receives from their God the daily bread that they need to sustain life. The gift of manna is enough for one day. Anything more that is gathered spoils. Provision is made for the sabbath, but beyond that each was to gather only what was needed, no more and no less (v. 18). The work that has the sabbath rest as its boundary is meant to sustain life, including that of fellow creatures, as the commandment insists.

25. Ibid., 131f.; cf. also 83, 90f., 167.

The institution of the sabbath draws attention to the fact that all creatures owe their life to God and it thus gives work the criterion of providing what is needed for life. The range of work is not so narrowly drawn as the story of the manna might suggest; we do not work merely to produce that which makes life's continuation possible. Just because the participation of work in God's rest gives it its criterion, work embraces all creaturely life. This activity is thus no less richly varied than in Aristotle's vivid description of the many forms of the active life. The only point is that the commandment, unlike Aristotle's ethics, adds rest to work. To the opposites listed by Ecclesiastes we might make an addition: Work and rest also have their time. We cannot do both at once, but neither can be "in time" without the other: work that is oriented to what is necessary for life and hence also to all that other creatures need for it, and rest that is directed to the origin of life, that focuses wholly on God and on what he has done to make it possible for there to be life. The monastic rule "Pray and work" expresses the same thought. It thus sums up the whole of human life before God and on behalf of creation. Prayer is part of work because it does not create anything but sees itself referred to the Creator's will in everything that comes to expression in complaint, petition, thanksgiving, and praise. The rest that follows work and gives it its proper criterion again is not said to be functional here, namely, as recreation that workers need so that when rested they can work all the better again. Nor is work understood simply as a means to achieve leisure. It is not a necessary evil that we must accept for the sake of the real living that we can attain to after it. Finally, work does not take place in the freedom of the creative self-fulfillment that might say in every form of activity: "This is where we are, and may be, truly human!"

That freedom, as distinct from working within the limits of creation, would be the motive for action that sees itself as meaningful work simply because in it we are self-determinative in all respects. Work for every purpose and in every form would then have to be creative. In it we supposedly move out of ourselves and find ourselves again by turning to what is outside us and appropriating it. Working, we become different. We enter a world without order, or a world that needs to be given shape, in order that we might recognize ourselves in what we do. Creative work brings together those who act and the objects of their action, the subjects that give meaning and disparate matter. It reconciles humanity to nature. This view of work, reflected philosophically in German Idealism and its heirs, in Fichte, Hegel, and Marx, evokes the question of meaning and builds on it. It thus reduces all activity to the giving of meaning by which reality without order (and we cannot properly call it reality because our senses perceive it as unstructured confusion and chaos) becomes reality for us, or, more strictly, is made reality for us. Everything, then, depends on that meaning of work by which all activity is measured and which can find satisfaction in no result so long as the world is not in the full sense the home of humanity.

For humans at work, however, the world is something that confronts them. That is an implication of the demand for meaning that is raised in all work. Work must provide that which things lack before our creative intervention, namely, the integration and arrangement of all elements in a meaningful context. Where reality is meaningfully ordered, it is due to the subject, whether individual or society. Subjectivity is the origin and center of all meaning even when meaning is defined as the form in which human experience is ordered[26] and hence does not derive from action alone. All perception becomes an achieving of order that gives meaning, and all work refers back to the active potential with which subjectivity tackles a world without shape.[27] Especially in modern utopias actions to change the world receive their meaning from the fact that they aim at a future fullness of meaning that we cannot anticipate — a fullness that revolutionary processes transform and direct to their

26. Luhmann, "Sinn als Grundbegriff," 3f. and 6.

27. I am indebted here to conversations with S. Müller (Augsburg, n.d.) and to his studies "Perspektivität der Erkenntnis und Perspektivität des Willens . . . ," in *Friedrich Nietzsche: Perspektivität und Tiefe,* ed. W. Gebhard (Frankfurt and Bern, 1962), 15ff.; and *Arbeit: Zur philosophischen Erhellung ihrer neuzeitlichen Genesis* (Freiburg and Munich, n.d.). For M. Heidegger, too, meaning is rooted in subjectivity. In his hermeneutics as exposition of human existence, notwithstanding all criticism of the subjection of the living world to objectifying work, he holds fast to the thesis that meaning must first be actualized by understanding as the basic action. What may be articulated in an understanding disclosure, we call meaning. This term embraces the formal scaffolding of what belongs necessarily to that which understanding exposition articulates. Meaning has and sees and grasps beforehand the structured whither of the design that makes something understandable as something. Cf. *Being and Time* (New York, 1962); and on Heidegger, P. Hofmann, *Metaphysik oder verstehende Sinn-Wissenschaft? Gedanken zur Neugründung der Philosophie im Hinblick auf Heideggers 'Sein und Zeit,'* Kant Studien suppl. 64 (Berlin, 1929).

own limited purposes. At the present stage of unfulfilled meaning and distant utopia it is actions that, as they are performed, guarantee the promise of meaning. All such views pose the question of meaning because they begin with the assumption that meaning is not intrinsic to the world (as Aristotle assumed it to be when he appealed to the *logos*) but has to be impressed upon it. As regards meaning, the world is unfinished. It can achieve completion only with the project of history.

Some variations of the motif of creative work show how far creation is pushed into the background. Helmut Gollwitzer bases the meaning of such work on the incomplete history of creation that makes the created world both a gift and a task, that is, the task of cooperating with the Creator in the fulfilling of his will.[28] God's verdict on his work is now a demand for meaning which sets it to work (we shall discuss this later in chap. IX). The goodness of the world is a claim made upon the world as it is. As God's Spirit hovered over the primal flood (Gen. 1:2), so the meaning of creation stands over a world that is virtually without meaning or threatened in its meaning. Jürgen Moltmann sounds a similar note when, as noted above, he not only finds the eschatological meaning of work but also, in the same breath, the meaning of society in historical communication with nature in the fact that we are called to cooperate with the God who creates and redeems.[29] The world here is the foundation for the coming kingdom of God, the stuff for the salvation that is to be attained.

Can we answer the question of meaning of work along these lines? Can we silence in this way the complaint about meaningless work and the threatened meaning of life? So much work in our society that allocates work seems to be meaningless because it is not perceived to be meaningful. Sociologists are right at this point. The relations of too many things are not seen or are not clear. We cannot measure their effects or results, let alone evaluate them. Individuals can no longer see where the detailed working steps are leading. Who then in their many different jobs can say responsibly whether what they do is providing what is essential for life? To proclaim at this point that work has an

---

28. H. Gollwitzer, *Krummes Kreuz — aufrechter Gang: Zur Frage nach den Sinn des Lebens* (Munich, 1970), 220-28, 309-13; and cf. idem, *Ich frage nach dem Sinn des Lebens* (Munich).

29. See 16 and n. 23.

all-embracing meaning is of little help. To say even that it cooperates in redemption is to burden everyday action or inaction in an intolerable way. It is more fitting to define the meaningfulness of all our activity as broadly and precisely as possible so that we may see its purpose and if it is ethically dubious make the right choice. Whether an action has meaning is in the first instance a question of its reference to objective meaning and then above all of its value for life in society and in creation as a whole.

But who knows what this value is? And how can individuals share in defining it so as to be able to share in responsibility as well? This is now the further and more radical question of the meaning of work. Can we simply give a practical reply in terms of the sociological establishment of a meaningful nexus of life, of the theory of the positing of meaning that declares such work to be basic and therefore necessary to life? The sabbath commandment, by not letting work be an elixir, contains clearer standards and also more cogent grounds for criticism than can be promised by a meaning of work that comprehends world history. What is commanded is simply that we should remain in the creation of God in which God gives us not only life but also what is needed for it. To stay within the limits of this creation is not the same as sustaining or even redeeming it. We can enjoy it and seriously imperil it, but can we wrest full control from it even in all the things that we destroy?

Christian theology denies this with its thesis of continuing creation, God's ongoing creative work. This is the touchstone for the question of the meaning of action.[30] Ecclesiastes replied that we cannot see the context of life, God's work from beginning to end. "He has made everything suitable in its time" (3:11). "God seeks out what has gone by" (v. 15). He holds possibilities in his hand and causes them to become realities again. But between this ongoing work and things and perceptible processes in time is a relation that we can neither see nor grasp. God is now hidden as Creator, hence nothing falls from his hand and we may experience and suffer and do what is definite. To try to say more

---

30. Luhmann discusses continuous creation in *Funktion der Religion*, 216; and in *Gesellschaftsstruktur und Semantik*, 268ff. His criticism is that it leads back simply to the question of contingency: Why thus and not otherwise? But only trust in God's faithfulness can answer this question. By its very nature this trust is not a mastering of contingency but expresses gratitude for the life that is given and leaves open what has to be left open.

about this would mean less, either anticipating the judgment of God or subjecting us to the power of the factual, either missing the faithfulness of God or so projecting the divine goodness into our lives that we are denied unexpected joy in what we are granted.

In all this Ecclesiastes not only speaks a different language but has in view something totally different from a creation that is translated into world history, into the process of world development. Behind that view is a loss of creation that must be made good by various means of giving and establishing meaning, or, in general, by the constructing of a meaningful context for life. Meaning becomes the theme when we lose open awareness of the gracious constitution of the world as creation and we experience finitude only in dissociation. A union of disparate elements now seems to succeed only by integrating and housing them in history. Historical and social reality is now saturated to the point of having it say itself what its basis is. It replies to this question of its origin by referring back in all its phenomena to the grounds of its development.

With this reconstruction sociology has taken up the philosophical and metaphysical riddle of the meaning of the existence of the world and solved it in its own way. Its formal definition of meaning as the form that gives order to human experience (Luhmann) seems to be so broad that it allows us to include all perceptions, even the perception of objective meaning at which Ecclesiastes stops. This definition, however, leads on smoothly to the theory of the establishing of meaningful contexts for life. Ecclesiastes found a break here that certainly raised further questions but that prevented him from making God's verdict on that which takes place with objective meaning in time into a perspective on our own action. He referred to something beyond our own experience, suffering, and action that we cannot comprehend as the basic meaning of all active encounter with the world, and only in this way could he inquire into the meaning of individual experiences and actions, that is, into their objective meaning, and especially into the right time for them in which they could take place in harmony with God's will.

This is how trust in creation expresses itself: All things come from God, but we cannot trace them back to him in such a way as to be able to explain and justify them. The question of meaning that seeks to establish the context of all meaningful actions speaks differently. In the view of those who put this question the world reflects itself as a broad web of meaning embracing what is accidental and what is necessary, what is indefinite and what is definable, classifying and structuring. It thus presses beyond the human need for orientation and expresses the need for justification with which we seek to give validity to our own lives when we no longer know any other court of last appeal for our life and action.

V. GENEALOGY OF THE QUESTION: MEANING OF HISTORY AND SUFFERING

W E ARE now at the provisional end of a path that has led us increasingly away from elementary perceptions. All the senses were finally harnessed as shaping forces to give the world reality. We must now show how this has given the question of meaning its profile.

We find one of the finest accounts of the path we have taken in the discussion of John 1:1 in Goethe's *Faust*. Faust finds written: "In the beginning was the Word," but saw no help there. He could not rate "word" so highly. With invocation of the Spirit's help he thus tried putting "meaning" for "word," but this would not do. Next he tried "power," but he could not stop at that. He finally fixed on *Tat* ("deed" or "act"):

> Mir hilfe der Geist! auf einmal sah ich Rat
> Und schreibe getrost: Im Anfang war die Tat![1]

In thus taking up the ancient philosophical question of origins, does Goethe put the answers in their proper historical sequence? The question of meaning long ago renounced confidence in deed as the origin and basis of reality! It is part of the crabwise gait of modern cultural history in the West that if we dismissed mere "word" and had to begin

---

1. Goethe, *Faust* I, vv. 1224, 1234.

with "meaning,"[2] the will behind the world had to follow behind meaning, and finally the basic act would be needed to give orderly structure to the world, yet meaning would then reemerge from neglect to reply to the question what basis there is for the active positing of the world.

The crisis of meaning that emerged and that showed itself to be a crisis in the orderly fashioning of the world was traced back by Friedrich Nietzsche to an increasing loss of sensory ability to perceive the world. The senses had to wither away in order to give place to the meaning of cosmic history and destiny. This meaning is sought behind and above the cosmos. It is set above the world in order that guided by it we might intervene in the world, having placed ourselves above it. Nevertheless, once we are no longer content simply to live in the world or to be exposed to the incomprehensibility of existence, the question of meaning confronts us. But first new and artificial senses develop, since the natural senses no longer seem adequate.

To the five senses we have added especially the sense of history. This instrument can change as history itself does. It arises out of the intrinsically disorderly and often enough obscure course of history and promises us a better view of things than the world of natural life can manage. In the section on first and last things, the first main section of part I of his *Human, All Too Human,* Nietzsche sees this sense at odds with the classical philosophical certainty that would derive what is eternally valid from what now is. A lack of historical sense was for him the hereditary failing of all philosophers. Many of them even blindly take the latest form of humanity, as it has arisen under the impact of specific religions and political events, as the fixed form with which we must begin. They are not prepared to learn that humanity has developed and that its capacity for knowledge has also developed.[3] We read again in *Die fröhliche Wissenschaft* that we can measure the degree of historical sense that an age possesses by the translations it makes and its attempts to make past ages and books its own.[4] This might sound very confident, displaying a high sense of the possibilities of extending the range of our own

2. Grimm, *Deutsches Wörterbuch,* X/1, 1148; and E. Jockers, "Im Anfang war die Tat?" *Mit Goethe: Gesammelte Aufsätze* (Heidelberg, 1957), 193ff.

3. F. Nietzsche, *Werke in drei Bänden,* ed. K. Schlechta (Darmstadt, 1963), I, §I, 448.

4. Ibid., II, 91; also 687, where Nietzsche says the 19th century knew this as its sixth sense; cf. *Beyond Good and Evil* (ET Edinburgh, 1909), 167.

experiences, of finding enrichment through history, and of seeing in what is past and strange more than what we ourselves already are. A little later, however, we find the unruffled section on the use of the historical sense,[5] which turns out to be a distinctive feature of our own age, its virtue and its sickness. Those who can feel all history to be their own history experience in a terribly generalized way all the affliction of the sick who think of health, of the aged who think of youthful dreams.[6] The historical sense means that those who have it can no longer forget anything.

This sense has little or nothing to do with the feeling for tradition in which a people, culture, or religion lives. Preceding it is the spirit of antiquarian research[7] that seeks to gather treasures that are no longer brought forth from the full sense of a fruitful present. The historical sense wants to make its own things that do not originally belong to it. It assimilates what has been brought forth earlier with a view to changing it. It does not view what has been as over and done with but as a tomb from which facts can arise as new possibilities. The world that the historical sense opens up as history is in general turned back into possibilities that simply await actualization. We may thus call this sense the sense of the possible. If there is a sense of the real there must also be a sense of the possible, says Rober Musil,[8] though not, of course, with reference to history alone, but with reference to the world as a whole, yet a world that lives solely on its fullness of possibilities. The sense of the possible grasps the world that Ecclesiastes called ongoing creation: "That which is, already has been; that which is to be, already is; and God seeks out what has gone by" (3:15). What we now read is that it is reality that awakens possibilities, and nothing would be more perverse than to deny that. Nevertheless, in sum or on average the same possibilities persist, repeating themselves until people come along who no longer think of something real as just that. These are the people who give possibilities their meaning and specificity, who bring them to life.[9] In this way the world becomes the denominator for meaning, which first brings reality to light and makes sense of it.

5. *Werke,* II, 92.
6. Ibid., 197f.
7. Ibid., 92.
8. R. Musil, *Der Mann ohne Eigenschaften,* vol. I (1930; repr. Hamburg, 1970), 16.
9. Ibid., 17.

Nietzsche also refers to the sense of suffering that arises through grief and pain. It was for him the harmful legacy of Christianity to teach us not to accept suffering as an unavoidable part of existence but to try to explain it. The helpless become sublimely active, raising the question of the meaning of suffering. They turn their impotent will away from the reality they suffer to an inner world to which they give breadth and depth by self-edification through suffering.

Apart from the ascetic ideal, Nietsche argued, "animal" humans had no meaning. Their existence on earth had no goal. Why they exist was a question with no answer. No will lay behind them or behind the earth. "In vain" was a refrain behind all great human destinies. The interpretation of the ascetic ideal was that something was lacking, that there was for us a great gap. We could not justify, explain, or affirm ourselves. We suffered in vain. We were in the main no more than sick animals. But suffering itself was not the real problem. The problem was the lack of any answer to the cry: Why do we suffer? As the bravest animals who are most used to suffering, we do not negate it, we want it, we seek it, presupposing that we can be shown some reason or purpose for it. The meaninglessness of suffering, not suffering itself, was the curse that previously lay over humanity. And the ascetic ideal offered a meaning. It explained suffering. It seemed to fill the monstrous gap. The door closed against self-destructive nihilism. The explanation undoubtedly brought new suffering with it, suffering more profound, more inward, more poisonous, more corrosive to life. It put all suffering under the perspective of guilt. Nevertheless, it offered redemption. It gave us meaning. We were no longer like leaves in the wind, playthings of meaninglessness, of nonsense. We could now will things, no matter, in the first instance, to what end or with what means. The will was rescued.[10]

For the moment let us leave Nietzsche's complaint against a theology of suffering on one side, the theology that by giving meaning to what is meaningless offers human existence its own justification. Let us first note how the word *meaning* has here taken on a different sense. It is a summary term for the mastering of life that can explain a suffering existence, that views it, then, as a text that we have written for ourselves. This meaning deadens the senses that feel pain by means of its own manufactured question as to the purpose of suffering. But it also causes

10. Nietzsche, *Werke*, II, 899f.; cf. 809f.

more pain by dealing with suffering, enhancing it to an immeasurable degree. But ought not our human sense to gather together and orient the senses without suppressing them in this way? Can it find in suffering only the lack of an answer that impels us to seek a purpose that will supply an answer? Nietzsche did not carry his thinking to this point, but this is the question that shows itself to be inescapable precisely in virtue of the question of meaning.

Nietzsche goes on to argue that the multiplying of our senses does not merely extend our range of perception but involves the association of the new senses with the others in a way that entails the subjection of the others. Common to both the sense of history and the sense of suffering is that they are interpretive senses that promise to give direction to perceptions without substituting for them. Interpretation, significance, and illusion may be registered as given but not definitively distinguished. All our senses are subject to deception.[11] This is because they do not merely impart perceptions but are also productive. To correct, to compare with what is similar or the same — the same process that any sense impression goes through — is a development of reason.[12] This observation links hermeneutics to physiology.

For Nietzsche the relating of sense perceptions to the interpretation of reality is a process of Western development in which Christianity played a large part and which is now at a crossroads at which hermeneutics and physiology are parting company. This is why we are disoriented and have come to speak about the question of the meaning of existence. Those who put this question cannot be content with their need for orientation but need to justify their existence so as to be sure where they stand. The Christian explanation of life has tried to meet this need for justification, but Christianity has now done as much as it can do in this direction. In rejecting the Christian interpretation and treating the meaning it offers as counterfeit, we come up in a terrible way against the question of Schopenhauer: Has existence, then, any meaning at all? This is a question, Nietzsche thought, that will need a few centuries to be heard fully and in all its profundity.[13] His prophecy was wrong only in the sense that a few

11. Ibid., III, 548.
12. Ibid., 729.
13. Ibid., II, 228.

decades were enough to make the question of meaning predominant even in the house of learning.

Nietzsche blamed Christianity for estranging us from direct perception of things and putting in its place "a world for humanity" that would be constructed by means of a network of meaning.[13] Meaning is the means of constructing this world as the link between us and reality. The objectivity of things, including events and history, is absorbed into this medium. We become progressively dependent on it as we learn to know ourselves as creatures in need of meaning. Those who cannot impose their will on things, those who are without will or power, do at least give them meaning, that is, the belief that a will is already there. A measure of the power of will is how far we can do without meaning in things, how far we are able to survive in a meaningless world because we ourselves organize a little part of it.[14]

Nietzsche thus sees the world divided into nature, which does not tell us what is the purpose of everything, and manufactured life, to which we have given meaning, and must continually give meaning, by our own will. As the organized world in distinction from the cosmos, human history arises. This is the place of the question of the meaning of existence and of the answers to this question that have already been given or are possible. It is important to keep in mind that Nietzsche will allow the question of meaning only insofar as we do not shrink from natural meaninglessness or try to master it inwardly by interpretation. Only then can the will, not having been lulled to sleep by impotent interpretations, go into action, and it can begin to work only as it sets its own goals and sees to their implementation. This point makes clear that Nietzsche is passionately fighting the work of interpretation, which is for him the origin of the question of meaning, only because it is a rival to the power of the will and compensates for a weakness of will. The organizing and creative will has to have a *telos* and hence a relation to meaning. But the meaning is not given; it is self-imposed. The significance is not assigned or forced but under control. Only the unconditioned will that is simply left to its natural freedom as regards meaning can shape the world on the premise that it does not already have any meaning. In other words, the question of meaning differentiates the old world from the new. Our new world: we have to recognize to what extent we are the creators of our sense of values

14. Ibid., III, 552, and for the first part of the sentence, II, 945.

and can thus posit meaning in history.[15] To what extent! This phrase gives Nietzsche pause, and by it he issues a warning against any total power over history, which would be an illusion. Nevertheless, the accents are on the creative ability that lifts us out of nihilism. Only on the basis of the experience that the whole is without meaning is history possible as the giving of meaning to what is meaningless. This is how Theodor Lessing would later describe it.[16]

The thinking of Nietzsche that the question of meaning rules out creation and makes us creators is something that we will have to take up again in chapter IX. We will now follow his thesis further with the help of the concepts of attempting and achieving interpretation that accompany the question of meaning.

History has been called a never-ending human mythicizing. It is born out of consoling self-cures for human need and unavoidable projections of it in wishes or ideals.[17] That is the verdict of Theodor Lessing along thoroughgoing Nietzschean lines. The basis for all that happens and for all explanations of it is human need. Any changing of an existing situation is under necessity, that is, the compulsion to avert a need.[18] Lessing wrote this under the impact of World War I, but it expresses the mood of the age that led to the war. His formula for giving meaning to what is meaningless is *logificatio post festum*,[19] that is, the subsequent establishment of order that brings to light the *logos* or meaning of what has happened. This formula reads like a manual for the many speculative views of the meaning of history, both religious and political, which have held the stage since the beginning of the twentieth century. The meaning of history has to help us to recapture the total context, which has been lost in actual conflicts.[20]

Not always is meaning so emphatic as in Lessing, for whom the offering of meaning tackles guilt and provides exculpation — with practical consequences that may be seen in many of the historical writings of the last

15. Ibid., 918.

16. T. Lessing, *Geschichte als Sinngebung des Sinnlosen oder die Geburt der Geschichte aus dem Mythos* (Munich, 1920; 4th ed., Leipzig, 1927).

17. Ibid., 3.

18. Ibid., 237.

19. Ibid., 237ff.

20. E.g., N. Berdyaev; and K. Jaspers, *Von Ursprung und Ziel der Geschichte*, 3rd ed. (Munich and Zurich, 1952).

decades, in which, on closer inspection, we find a rewriting of history. One who knows historicism like Friedrich Meinecke holds aloof from such wrestings of history. Meinecke inquired into the view of the historical world as a stream of infinite development that gained dominance from the eighteenth century onward.[21] In contrast to the monumental claims to be giving meaning to world history that were made in the 1930s as proof of a historical sense, he boasted that he himself was drawing attention to the transcendent meaning of history. Through historical phenomena historical meaning promotes individual humanity and shows how this demonstrates itself in its commitment to action in pure humanity.

There is no direct reference to the meaning of suffering here, but the indirect reference is all the more cogent. We see ourselves surrounded by an immeasurable fullness of causal relations, of necessities which do not promise to avert any need but to abolish freedom, and in that way to set aside an essential human need, namely, the venture of free decision. Necessities tell us that we can act only in accordance with their meaning, in acceptance of what is. In so doing, they say, we may act fruitfully and need not ask why or to what purpose. The question of meaning arises out of pain at this fatalism as it confronts us in the garb of complete causal explanations of human life. It opposes the flight into circumstances with which we try to excuse ourselves because we will not accept the guilt that is inescapably linked to freedom. Meaning has to do with the question whether we will accept ourselves in our inalienable individuality.

The question of the meaning of history arose when the mere recalling of an ideal or idealized past proved just as fragile as the optimistic belief in progress. Both were at odds with the experience of the present that can find a place only when we do not rely on either our origin or our future, which we can never truly know. Who knows where we are going? We hardly remember whence we came. Meinecke recalls the quotation to this effect from Goethe's *Dichtung and Wahrheit*[22] — a fresh variant on the question of the meaning of existence. This question must no longer burden us if we are to rise above the circumstances and

---

21. F. Meinecke, "Geschichte und Gegenwart" (1933), in *Vom geschichtlichen Sinn und vom Sinn der Geschichte*, 3rd ed. (Leipzig, 1939), 18. The essays collected in this work are sidepieces to Meinecke's work *Historism: The Rise of a New Historical Outlook* (ET New York, 1972).

22. Meinecke, "Geschichte und Gegenwart," 10.

forces that seem to control us. The historical sense comes into play at this point. As Meinecke sees it, this sense detects in all forms of humanity traces of eternity.[23] To inquire into meaning means leaving the empirical context of becoming and facing the claim of the absolute, the divine. This expresses itself in the demand that conscience makes on individuals to exist and act unconditionally, without regard to seen causes and results that are naturally present and important, but that cannot sustain humanity. The question of the meaning of history creatively breaks through the causal chain in order that individuality may relate directly to the eternal. None of us can measure the meaning of history as a whole, but we can all be bearers of meaning by adopting an absolute standpoint, that is, by adopting a standpoint vis-à-vis the absolute.

This idealistic view stands opposed to Nietzsche's nihilism and therefore in creative tension with it. In both cases meaning is the antithesis of a nonhuman rationality and of all thoroughgoing rational explanations of the world. Meaning arises prior to all reason and it stands above reason. It is the place of origin for humanity. It makes all that is present into a task or demand that we should be fully human and not be driven by necessities or use them as excuses for ourselves. All historical constructs, all traditions and institutions, become media for the claim that is made upon us, whether from the absolute or from the needs of our own existence, that we should intervene in historical occurrence. Traditions and factors such as nation, state, religion, and culture are there afresh at our disposal. This can mean either their dissolution or an opportunity with their help to achieve again the harmony of personal destinies with the suprapersonal world. The question of meaning works like a ferment in all the historical phenomena that constantly hold out promise of coming into being. For creative individuals and human societies it changes these into occasions for the establishment of a true historical context if we accept the responsibility. This is how another advocate of historicism, Ernst Troeltsch, depicted a way of dealing with history on the basis of its suprahistorical, metaphysical roots, namely, as an interpretation of its meaning that leads to the judgment that sees the continuity of history and continues it as a relatively creative act.[24]

23. Ibid., 18f. and 21.
24. E. Troeltsch, "Modern Philosophy of History," in *Religion and History* (ET Minneapolis, 1991), 316.

Meinecke wanted to reawaken the sense of history at a time and in a situation in which the demand was for the absolute commitment of individuals to a common cause. Those who have ears to hear can hear that this meaning is intended as a warning against appealing to providence, nationality, or other supraindividual forces in order to escape the counterquestion of right and wrong. The historical sense immerses itself in what was once humanly possible. As Nietzsche observed, it can thus become resigned. But it can equally well take courage and display prudence when it recalls the limits of the human instead of taking flight into what is above the human. This is the view of Meinecke and many who think like him when he calls the meaning of history a mystery that eludes our advance knowledge and yet discloses its "meaning for us."[25] That takes place when we do not try to withdraw by means of explanations of the whence and whither but do what has to be done unconditionally here and now.

Similar voices make themselves heard particularly in crisis, for example, face-to-face with the existential threat to a people (as when the state of Israel was being set up), or in situations of upheaval. They can help to warn us not to accept a total meaning for history that explains what has happened or what has to happen by means of certain fixed formulas, for then we need only do what is prescribed for us by the previous survey. The meaning of history for us can also set aside the meaning of individual life by absorbing it into a historical task. There are plenty of examples of this both past and present. We no longer ask after the meaning of life when existence as a whole seems to be at risk, when it is not just under threat but may be secured or lost. The destiny of individuals can no longer be subject to the question of good and bad when everything is to be decided already by a life's task.

The historical sense and the question of the meaning of history can work out in very different ways. The sense of the absolute within all the relativity, of that which persists in time, is sharpened by pain at transitoriness and all the explanations of it. Interest in what is comparable, in correspondences and common features that we find in the flow of events, feeds on suffering from constant parting, the only thing that seems to persist. All this may help us to stand up to events and to ward off the power of the factual that threatens to beat down all our human

25. Meinecke, "Geschichte und Gegenwart," 22.

questioning. But it may also produce a greater recklessness that does not worry about the results of what we do because it regards these as unimportant compared to what is achieved at the "decisive moment." A verdict on ultimate motivations is hardly possible. The historical sense certainly cannot attain to it. Here again it shows itself to be ambivalent. It may motivate flight into the irrationality of positing values, and deeds done in the name of these can then easily become the offspring of a human establishing of the self in history, and look confused to the organization of the world by the will that Nietzsche propagated. Or else the historical sense respects the human mystery as in what we do or do not do we bear witness to the fact that our experience and action are not self-explanatory.

Finally, the historical sense rests on interpretations. Troeltsch claimed as interpretation his judgment that a total historical context can be discovered and developed. He did not mean by this interpreting events in relation to their future importance by unveiling history as the interrelated and unbroken manifestation of the absolute, or, in theological terms, as the history of divine revelation and the revelation of history.[26] But even this can be taken in at least two ways. Either the total context is conceivable only on the premise that nothing is left out because in some manner everything has to do with the divine. In this case, however, everything is in a higher sense indifferent and the only decisive thing is to see each and every thing in relation. Or else the continuity of history depends on the linkage and persistence of actualized values and its meaning derives from cultural development. But since thus far this has not proceeded in a uniform way, the interpretation of this meaning becomes a means of setting off one culture against another, a weapon in holy wars on behalf of the superiority of one's own culture, and, as is well known, appealing to the meaning of history is very susceptible in this regard.

26. Cf. Troeltsch, "Historical and Dogmatic Method in Theology," in *Religion and History*, 316: the view of history as an evolving of divine reason; also *Gesammelte Schriften*, vol. III: *Der Historismus und seine Probleme* (Tübingen, 1922), 212: the relativity of values making sense only if an absolute is alive and at work in these relative things. Presupposed is a vital process of the absolute in which it can be grasped and shaped by each point in a way appropriate to that point. The different points must also relate to one another and succeed one another according to a specific rule that constitutes the essence of the coming into being of the divine Spirit and that still imposes itself in all contingencies and all the confusions and rejections of the will.

Where the historical sense has to consider what endures in some other way than tracing the sequence of causes and effects, namely, as meaning for the human spirit, it needs to be able to distinguish reality from appearance. Nietzsche doubted whether we can do this and thus wanted to unmask the question of the meaning of history as a mere question of power and survival. God had to be shut out of history lest any of us yield to the self-deception that may be a fruitful illusion regarding the whence and whither of life but that turns out to be a lie that evades the harshness of suffering.[27] Where history is the space-time to which we expose ourselves with our question as to the meaning of existence, the question of meaning arises. Historicism tried to answer it by enclosing God, as it were, in history, history being seen as open in two directions, that of divine penetration and that of unforseeable becoming.

Can religion support this answer or does the religious sense simply become a higher instrument of the question of meaning and possibly even of an unceasing questionability?

27. Cf. Nietzsche on interpreting history in honor of a divine reason, as constant testimony to a moral purpose and to moral ends; also on the decline of Christianity due to a morality (which is perpetual) that turns against the Christian God; the sense of truth which Christianity has highly developed is disgusted at the falsity and mendacity of the whole Christian world and its interpretation of history.

VI. THE RELIGIOUS SENSE?

THE TERM *meaning* has taken on religious (or, for Idealistic thinking, moral and religious) accents. The historical sense comes into contact with another nonsensory and supranatural sense that elevates it and pushes it to the limits. As we have noted,[1] Schleiermacher in the early nineteenth century described the feeling and taste for the infinite, the supreme sense, as religion. This sense is oriented to the infinite, and by this Schleiermacher meant *the* reality that we cannot attain to by any of the operations of active human experience or human thinking, since these have to do only with finite objects. First, then, the religious sense is characterized by the fact that it is wholly other than all the other senses. Only thus can it grasp what is hidden from the other senses, and to do this it must make itself independent of them. But who dare maintain, asks Schleiermacher in another context, that the consciousness of great and holy thoughts that the spirit engenders of itself depends on the body, or that our sense of the true world makes use of external members?[2] It is to our creative spirit, to what is God-related in us, that the true world opens itself, and this world is not only beyond all bodily reality but is in every place where the infinite is present in the finite, as shown by the fact that the finite points infinitely beyond itself. The religious

1. See p. 12 and n. 15.
2. Schleiermacher, *Soliloquies* (ET Chicago, 1926), 93.

sense is our feeling for incorruptibility, for that which finally lasts; hence it is itself incorruptible.

Religion, traced back to the religious sense, replaces what Christian theology calls faith. It does not view itself as just a name for piety in general, which Christian faith manifests only in one of many different forms. It also changes the nature of faith by freeing it from its traditional subjection to authority (the church and the Bible) and seeking to discover it afresh in terms of its origin, that is, as an immediate perception of the divine, as a feeling of absolute dependence, as Schleiermacher defines it,[3] which also carries with it a feeling of being totally sheltered and upheld. That upon which we may finally and most profoundly rely — that is the meaning about which no more can be said. No one can explain its nature. No one can describe it or derive it from anything else. It is one of the great basic and ultimate words that we can only tear apart if we try to explain them. It may be known only in its effects, in its meaning for us, as a foundation on which to rest as a final content, as significance that rests in itself. We can neither get behind it by reflection nor establish it by action. Both these must grow out of it if they are not to be without roots. It permits and demands only harmony with itself, which it attains to as it promises to fulfill our humanity.

I have said that the religious sense replaces faith by seeking to make it understandable afresh, and fundamentally, as basic trust in the meaning of the universe and confident reliance on the mystery of life. This sounds exhaustive, but it disguises the fact that the distinction between faith and superstition is lost here. If we translate faith totally into trust, it is not protected against trusting in an idol. Luther laid his finger on this point in his exposition of the first commandment: "I am the Lord your God . . . you shall have no other gods before me" (Exod. 20:2f.). "Question: What does it mean to have a God? Or what is God? Answer: A God is that from which we find provision of every benefit and refuge in all times of need. To have a God then is simply to trust and believe in him with all one's heart, as I have often said that only the trust and belief of the heart make both God and idol."[4] The longing for confidence can create a God for itself; its demand can become obvious to it, and it may thus infer that it has a basis that it calls God. But this is a God

3. Schleiermacher, *The Christian Faith* (ET Edinburgh, 1928), §4.
4. Luther's Large Catechism, WA, XXX/1, 132f.

without name whom we cannot invoke and who cannot reply but who has a relation to those who trust only in the form of a dialogue with the self.

The religious sense can hardly distinguish between God and idol because the sense with which it feels has nothing to say on this point. The religious sense plunges itself into the all-embracing whole. Its opposite is simply emptiness, absence of either basis or relation. It can be measured by nothing above or outside it. It can thus be described only in terms of its functions. It grants confidence and shelter; it overcomes alienation and distance. Those who would question it do not know what else to ask because it is the source of all the questions that can be answered. None of us as long as we live can dispense with the religious sense in this absolute and anonymous form. The religious sense, as faith, grants us our original relationship which some people may not see at times but out of which we cannot fall.[5] The salvation of this sense (as faith) is that of confidence. For "sense" is simply what is given, the refuge for all experience, the saving power for people in a disrupted world who have fallen in and with all that is around them.

Schleiermacher himself plainly did not intend to go that far when he commended religion to his contemporaries as a sense and taste for the infinite, to contemporaries who had lost themselves in the world of phenomena and forgotten the true world in the process. The usage that I have tried to sketch developed only, if I am right, in the century after him. Today, however, it has become so self-evident that hardly any of us ask how it really was that earlier usage was quite different. The question previously was not that of the meaning of life but of salvation or perdition, of right or wrong, of forgiveness or guilt. Meaning was

5. For example, V. Frankl, "Gegenwartsprobleme der Psychotherapie," *Die Sinnfrage in der Psychotherapie*, ed. N. Petrilowitsch (Darmstadt, 1972), 375. We have to accept this meaning because we cannot get behind it, for in the attempt to answer the question of meaning in terms of being we always have to presuppose the being of meaning. See also B. Welte, *Auf der Spur des Ewigen* (Freiburg im Breisgau, n.d.), 23: "Grasping meaning as an active grasping of my possible agreement with my whole being as agreement with the whole of being, the basic action that alone gives any possible reason for detailed action. As this process is thus the most original, it is also the most comprehensive, uniting me as a whole to being as a whole. It is the secret but for that reason all the more effective philosophy that stands at the beginning of all our thoughts and words and ways."

not sought and experienced in suffering but in consolation.[6] The concern was not with the meaning of work but with vocation and state of life and the respective duties. The question of the final meaning of the world had not yet replaced expectation of God's final action as Judge and Savior. The word *meaning* in the final sense that is of so much interest to us was obviously dispensable. Before we seek reasons for the crisis of meaning that has developed we should be clear what has been gradually ascribed to the concept. We shall find there the background of the threat that is a subject of such loud complaint today. I will limit myself to a few features that I regard as particularly significant.

Leading religious theoreticians in the late nineteenth and the early twentieth century such as Troeltsch and Rudolf Otto understood by "infinity" the whole of religious reality, and therefore what Otto would call a religious sensitiveness relates to the "eternal meaning" of reality as a whole.[7] "Religious" has to do with a total view of the universe. It thus strives to knit together in one all sense perceptions and all reflection.[8] The religious sense points to the destructive splintering of all experience caused by the rift between spirit and nature, reason and feeling, learning and life. To be sure, religion, too, has to do with a special experience. Troeltsch calls this the achieving of awareness of the order of the world of experience,[9] while Otto speaks of a shattering by the divine that lifts us above ourselves. Both of these are basic experiences that integrate all further experience and action and have the whole of reality as their content.

Often, then, "meaning" is simply an emphatic expression for the whole, not as something incalculable but the whole that is now present

---

6. Cf. K. I. Nitzsch, *Praktische Theologie,* vol. III/1 (Bonn, 1857), 171; and on this F. Wintzer, "Sinn und Erfahrung Probleme und Wege der Krankenseelsorge," in *Theologie und Wirklichkeit,* ed. H. W. Schütte and F. Wintzer (Göttingen, 1974), 213n.8.

7. R. Otto, "Naturwissenschaft und Theologie . . . ," in H. W. Schütte, *Religion und Christentum in der Theologie Rudolf Ottos* (Berlin, 1969), 122 (thesis II.5); and cf. 39 for the ambivalent term *Ahndung.*

8. See H. Braeunlich, "Das Verhältnis von Religion und Theologie in Ernst Troeltsch und Rudolf Otto: Untersuchungen zur Funktion der Religion als Begründung der Theologie" (diss., Bonn, 1979).

9. E. Troeltsch, *Psychologie und Erkenntnistheorie in der Religionswissenschaft: Eine Untersuchung über die Bedeutung der Kantischen Religionslehre für die heutige Religionswissenschaft* (Tübingen, 1905), 23; idem, "On the Question of the Religious A Priori," in *Religion in History* (ET Minneapolis, 1991), 39-40.

and salutary and sustaining. Here the question of meaning means openness to this whole. It contradicts the dissociation of our everyday world, especially of scientifically splintered and atomized reality, which may indeed be time and again reaffirmed and reorganized and rebuilt, but which is reduced to inert matter by such operations. In contrast, meaning represents the factor of life that can be analyzed only at the cost of its living quality. We can only feel this quality, not register it along understandable lines, for to be able to feel something is the whole meaning of life, as the poet Otto Flake wrote on the eve of World War I.[10] The word *meaning* has a power of suggestion which brings every secondary question whose goal is distinction that clarifies under the suspicion of unbelief, and even of hostility to humanity, or inhumanity. This is the religious signature of the question of meaning — not a theological one, for then we would have to speak not only of feeling and the lack of it, the equivalents of faith and unbelief, but also of faith in distinction from superstition.

Under the impact of the cultural crisis in and after World War I, Paul Tillich gave expression again to Nietzsche's shattering experience of the question of the meaning of existence, but this time expressly as the question of meaning. Nietzsche had put this question for the sake of truth. He had also issued a warning that it was better to leave it alone because it carries with it the danger of deception resulting from doubt as a radical will to know the truth. The more surprising, then, is the way in which Tillich equated the questions of meaning and truth when he said that doubters in religiously important questions are those who with the loss of religious immediacy to God have also lost the truth and the meaning of life or are at some point on the way that leads to this loss, yet who cannot remain content with the loss but are smitten with the demand that they find meaning, truth, and God. Doubters, then, are in the position of those who despair of salvation, except that for them the lack of salvation is not God's verdict of rejection but the abyss of lack of meaning.[11] As regards perdition the divine judgment and the abyss of meaninglessness are one and the same, so that it seems possible

10. B. B. Fischer, *Sie schrieben mir oder was aus meinem Poesiealbum wurde* (Munich, 1982), 66.

11. P. Tillich, *Rechtfertigung und Zweifel* (1924), in *Gesammelte Werke*, ed. R. Albrecht, vol. VIII: *Offenbarung und Glaube* (Stuttgart, 1970), 89.

that the question of meaning might be intelligibly presented as a secular version of the question of God. We need to see a basis of meaning that embraces history and the world of experience and that can be thought of as absolute. Finding such a basis justifies those who ask, for they come up against the presence of God in reality. God is present in many different ways, but always with the result that we are led further, whether by giving this historical moment an eternal content; by making a decisive moment in cultural development distinctive as *kairos*, as fulfilled time, and precisely in so doing giving new force to the constant task of actualizing values; by making it possible to think of God as the final unity of sensory forms that condition our knowledge and the meaningful contents that confront them as demands; or finally by teaching us to understand ourselves as the overarching unity of what we are and what we ought to be, of life as both a gift and a task.[12] God's presence will not leave the question of meaning undisturbed but raises it afresh, the need for orientation and the need for justification being very closely related.

Tillich, or the Idealistic legacy that he so cautiously represents, might well be the originator of the formulation in the basic program that I quoted at the outset: God as the basis of meaning and being. Truly we find expressed here in as succinct a way as we could desire everything that motivates and has had to motivate our contemporaries. The statement is both critical and yet it has also the form of an open question. The meaning of life has become questionable for us because we cannot grasp the depth or future of the world, or can do so only after the manner of a task that has still to be fulfilled. God, however, has not committed the world to human beings and left them to their own devices. In contents of meaning that are both gift and task he shows us in what direction we must orient ourselves. God reserves ultimate meaning for himself alone, but for that very reason the meaning accessible to us can be the pacemaker of being.[13] This implies that we must view our world and ourselves as not yet finished, not simply in the sense of

---

12. Tillich, *Gesammelte Werke,* vol. I: *Religionsphilosophie,* 318f.; idem, *Gesammelte Werke,* vol. VI: *Kairos,* 9ff.; idem, *Systematic Theology,* vol. I (Chicago, 1951), 66, etc.; II (1957), 78ff.

13. V. Frankl, "Aphoristische Bemerkungen zur Sinnproblematik" (1964), in *Die Sinnfrage in der Psychotherapie,* 417.

being incomplete but in the sense of being capable of development. Meaning embraces an incalculable openness of humanity and the world.

What is wrong with that? I must begin my reply by pointing out what is plainly not said in this wide-ranging conception, that is, that to which it is not open and against which it even shows itself to be immune. Unlike the religious sense, biblical religion speaks of God as Creator, Judge, and Savior. But we cannot talk in this way when we raise an apparently comprehensive question of God as the basis of meaning and being. The question of God seems to be more general than what the Bible specifically tells us about God. It promises access to an experience of God that is not linked to the Christian confession but may lead to it. Nevertheless, the question of God that is the motivation of life, even its elixir, for all who are truly alert, focuses simply and solely on that which comprises the relation of the world and humanity to God, the openness of meaning that leads being back to its basis and enables us to understand the world's direction. Even though there is strong emphasis on the fact that the world and humanity are questionable, this takes place in the interests of the fact that the question is worth putting, since it is not denied that the world and humanity derive from a meaning that only for the time being is hidden from us or misplaced. It may be said that all experience is always ambivalent because it never carries its final meaning within itself, or its meaning can be misunderstood or misused, but still all experience is positive in some way, for if it had no share in meaning we could not experience it, and if it had no sustaining significance it would not be subject to interpretation.

Along such lines the religious sense, even in its secularized form as the question of meaning, sees all reality as under the sign of grace. Grace implies a relation that is granted unconditionally and that cannot finally be lost. Uncertainty and doubt may indeed arise, but they are symptoms of a lack of clarity that spur on those who doubt to inquire further and in this way to leave uncertainty and doubt behind.

The despair of those who perish because God has rejected them is unknown to the question of meaning. It also knows nothing of the assaults that come upon those who suffer under silence of God, God having become alien to them even though they have heard his promise and staked their lives upon it. God's sentence of rejection has nothing whatever to do with the loss of meaning we may experience temporarily without falling victim to nothingness but in which we cannot stay forever if we are still to be human, since we are smitten with the demand that we find meaning, truth, and God. The remoteness of God for those who stand under his judgment is very different from the remoteness of final meaning from all experience of meaninglessness and of meaning that is only provisional and penultimate. God can cause human beings, things, and epochs to perish beyond recall. His remembering alone is the measure of historical remembrance. He does not posit a finitude that we might traverse with our questions but brings life and death to a definitive end. He is the Lord of life and death, not the sustainer of a universe in which everything, even life or death, finds its place and can stay in relationship. The religious question of meaning knows untruth only as the state of truth that is incomplete and perhaps even imperfect. In contrast, biblical and theological talk of God cannot ignore the falsehood with which we fully shut ourselves off from God. We curve in upon ourselves. We are not ready even for inward expansion. We hope to remain isolated and better protected this way. That we can never exclude or escape God is written on another page as our constitutional relationship with God that, as the question of meaning presupposes, we cannot abandon without falling out of the world.

The counterquestion might be raised, however: Are not God's redemption and judgment "meaning for us," the ways in which he enters into relation with us, redemption as the positive form, judgment as the critical, expressing grace on the one hand and wrath on the other, but both relations and therefore belonging together in God? And in this regard is not judgment a penultimate word in contrast to grace, included in the intention to show mercy, pain for the sake of healing? We might recall in this respect the prophetic summons to conversion in which the proclamation of judgment is designed to draw attention to God's ultimate will to save: "Have I any pleasure in the death of the wicked, says the Lord God, and not rather that they should turn from their ways and live?" (Ezek. 18:23).

It is true that in all we experience in encounter with him God has salvation and not perdition in view. "I know the plans I have for you, says the Lord, plans for your welfare and not for harm, to give you a future with hope" (Jer. 29:11). Nevertheless, promises of this kind do not permit us to bring God's action under the common denominator of a relation to him that simply takes different forms. If I previously had to protest against applying the concept of contingency to what we say about God, I must now affirm that judgment and salvation are in fact contingent insofar as they are what they are and so not something different. This means that God's grace and wrath express themselves in judgment and salvation in a way that prevents us from getting behind them to God himself. Similarly, the silence of God is not just the other side of his revelation. Both are ways in which God turns to us, and as such both point to the mystery of his freedom — his freedom to speak when and how he wills without our being able to deduce either his speech or his silence from a knowledge of his will. The relations that God sets up — but that, we see now, is too abstract, and instead we should say the judgment and redemption with which he encounters us — do not, when put together and expressed in terms of meaning, constitute God in his fullness, or, in other words, God in the unity of his person. Instead, judgment and redemption decide what it is that has standing and receives standing before God, what is called into life and what falls victim to death. If God's judgment does not totally destroy, this is not always foreseen already in his grace but is a free act of his faithfulness. If everything were finally grace, judgment would only be an episodic manifestation beyond which God himself would be bound to go. God's wrath would be the reverse side of his mercy, and it would have to be passing unless God were willing to make himself irrevocably poor.

The question of God, when translated into the question of meaning, leaves no place for talk of the revelation and silence of God. Looking for meaning as an eloquent relation, it adopts a position beyond any specific divine communication. It does not accept God's Word as a verdict on life and death. It views everything that can be said about God as a way of expressing the basic relation in which we find ourselves as long as we can ask, that is, as long as we can exist in a movement toward the positive. It is no longer God who himself communicates by his judgment the relation to the world and humanity in which we can live. The relation to God is mediated by the nexus of discovered and lived-out relations, the understanding of God being an integral part of these relations.

If faith is reduced to a relation of this kind, we see this from the fact that crises of faith even to the point of loss of faith can be made understandable as disruptions of relationship that may be dealt with therapeutically. For this reason the question of meaning plays an instructive role in psychotherapy,[14] and religious philosophers who take up the question see themselves as messengers of healing for the intellectual situation of their day. Healing is explained to be integration or a restoration of a harmony by way of balance. This, too, is an indication of a retreat from a theological view of healing as salvation, in which salvation as it applies to the whole, undivided person is not directed at the totality of humanity but at human beings as wholly God's work and as those who show to whom alone it is that they belong. Whether they are at one with themselves or with the world around them is another question. Salvation may well often lead precisely to alienation from an unsaved world, and reconciliation with God may not make a harmonious impact but may often evoke strong resistance and irreconcilable hostility. A religious sense that is thought of in terms of relationship cannot easily measure things of this kind. It sees everything in the light of grace and redemption. It is not a light without shadows, and to that extent it has to speak of sin as remoteness from fullness of meaning, but it is the basic and illuminating thing that makes possible the absorption of everything opposed to it into the nexus of meaning.

When it has a religious cast the question of meaning does not see the antithesis of grace and judgment or faith and unbelief. It seeks a meaning that gives health and life, for our reality is covered over with a network of artificial relations. Among these is the sequence of causes and effects that the historical sense already could accept as a worthy basis for explanation. We must also mention the many theories about humanity and its conduct that direct our experience with ourselves and others. These are meant to protect us against the risk of exposure to incalculable human encounters. Only the living relationship, however, has meaning. This cannot be put in a schema that reads it off from descriptions and generalizes it. We can know meaning in the true sense only from the requirement to be ourselves and to accept the other similarly as an incommensurable self. The scientific and pseudoscientific models that we impose on ourselves and others are a hindrance to self-experience. A sense of the concrete has to avoid abstractions of all kinds in order to open itself to the meaning of relationship that can never be made hard-and-fast or put at our instant disposal, but that grows out of living fellowship, the fellowship of the Thou and the world.

14. *Die Sinnfrage in der Psychotherapie.*

As Martin Buber put it, this sense grants us certainty that the meaning of existence is opened up and attainable in lived-out concreteness.[15] It raises the question of the meaning of life[16] by kindling a sense of the Thou[17] that finds the meaning of relationship in mutuality,[18] the dialogical constitution of reality. The meaning of relationship that grows out of encounter with God has to prove itself to the world.[19]

Buber's observations are meant to be read as contradicting any dealing with experiences that presents only artificial relations. Among these are attitudes that do not show a full involvement of one's own existence. Naturally those who begin with the experiencing of experience necessarily fail because they do damage to the spontaneity of the mystery. They alone attain to the meaning who accept the full sway of reality with no reservation or restraint and reply to it in a living way, that is, with full readiness to demonstrate the meaning in their lives. Meaning is found when we share in its manifestation by commitment of our own person.[20] In this way Buber takes up again the religious motif for which Schleiermacher had contended with his "feeling for the true world" in opposition to thinking and action that were torn away from the root soil of existence. Meaning here is that which is immediately original, and it can thus be found only when we look away from everything that might estrange us from the self. Forms of alienation are prepared or preconsidered experiences that make life subject, including activities in which we carry out only part of what is prescribed for us from outside, or by which we seek to accomplish something that no longer leaves any traces of the self. Wherever we do not commit the whole self, we are without feeling and reality is silent. We have here a picture of the sickness of a society that has become alien to reality no matter how much it may think it understands and controls everything, including expressions of its own life. The question of meaning is a cry of distress from those who can no longer tolerate the lack of relationship

15. M. Buber, *Eclipse of God: Studies in the Relation between Religion und Philosophy* (ET repr. New York, 1957), 14.

16. Buber, *I and Thou*, 2nd ed. (ET New York, 1958), 76.

17. Ibid., 54.

18. Ibid., 6.

19. Ibid., 80.

20. Buber, *Eclipse of God*, 14.

in which they are entangled. This at least is a diagnosis that judges the health of individual and social life by fulfilled relations. But here religious talk about meaning with its variations runs into a linguistic problem. Because radical antitheses have to be relied upon when it comes down to basics (fullness and emptiness, meaningful and meaningless, order and chaos, etc.), each time such talk must, as it were, have recourse to the totality. This is obviously best done by appealing to a feeling for the whole, a receptivity to what is final and basic and sustaining. Lest we should at once go that far, I will try to elucidate the meaning of relationship more closely by means of some obvious questions.

A glance at discussions within psychotherapy shows that the question of meaning here does not simply echo the complaint of contemporaries suffering from lack of meaning. The stress that is laid on sense experience as opposed to all nonexistential interpretations also gives evidence of a domestic debate. What is contested above all is the meaning that suffering in its various forms brings to light.

The healing of the most human of all sicknesses, self-sickness, depends on analysis of experience and is indeed part of the analysis of the nexus of experiences. How much life, especially the sick life, is viewed here as a text that has to be expounded may be seen from one of the classical cases of psychoanalysis, the history of the sickness of Freud's so-called Wolf-Man, who recalls that during the first months of analysis by Freud a whole new world opened up for him of which few at that time knew anything. Much that had made no sense in his life before acquired a meaning, and he now became conscious of connections that had previously been obscure to him.[21] Analysis has to do with the constructing of relationships of meaning. But it is not immediately clear whether these are life-constituted and have only to be disclosed or whether they are first constructed by interpretation and thus form the artificial scaffolding that the sick use to erect the meaning that they do not have.

However that may be, the life story is here a text that only an expert can decipher, and paradoxically it is specifically its author who does not know how to read it. Meaning here, hermeneutically, has the sense of a significant content that has to be brought to light by knowledge of the context. It can be known only when the context is known. This nexus

21. *The Wolf-Man* (ET New York, 1971).

of relationships is always present when life is understood hermeneutically. Sickness and health depend upon the degree of its disclosure and presence to the consciousness. The sick, whose natural and self-explanatory relationships are concealed from them, need meaning as a significant context that is disclosed. The relationships are destructive because they are not under control and they do not do properly what they are meant to do, that is, protect individual life at its personal center. For any possibility of healing, the distortion has to be brought to light, and above all the different elements have to be put in the right relationship to one another in which they can develop constructively.

Let us remember Freud's reservations regarding the question of meaning and value. He would accept it only as a manifestation of sickness.[22] It is not an issue where there is no friction but harmony between all the psychosomatic functions. In dealing with the deformation of meaning, with neurological closure to a healthy nexus of relationships, it becomes clear, however, that all of us stand in need of exposition. We can be healed only as we learn to communicate ourselves, and healing means a gradual and painful process of linguistic self-disclosure interrupted by many setbacks. Language proves to have healing power. It is not just a bearer of meaning, a carrier of information, but a medium for humanity, and also, of course, for its sickness. Psychoanalytical hermeneutics, for which the sick are books with many seals that have to be broken open, runs up against the fact that language can just as well conceal reality as reveal it. It can falsify. It can deceive both those who hear and those who speak. Yet we can be up to its tricks, for as our primal utterance it cannot just communicate anything but always communicates the speaker, too. In this fact consists not just the opportunity but also the burden of self-expression, for only rarely do we express ourselves without disguise. In psychoanalytical practice and theory meaning has a specific rank, not as the value that we all set for ourselves and seek to actualize, but as the significance that we all have; not as the special distinction that might lift us above others as important personalities, but as the content that we are forced to communicate over and above all the need for chatter. All of us have a significance to which we are sentenced, but it is only seldom that we succeed in expounding it for others or for ourselves. Meaning is always expounded significance.

22. See 13 and n. 16.

With this understanding of meaning psychoanalysis has consistently developed a hermeneutics that does not seek merely to explain texts but to unlock the whole world of human life by means of speech.

Suffering in soul draws attention to meaning as the significance that is to be derived from expressions of life and that impacts every human history in a way that can be interpreted. People are sick because they come up against encoded messages from the self that they cannot decipher, as in dreams or physical reactions. That they cannot escape in spite of all their efforts to do so is shown by the fact that in the long run we can none of us exist without some express and understandable meaning. We attain to this when in the context in which we find ourselves we stand in such a way that the relations to the construction of which we willy-nilly contribute are our own, are not alien to us or even hostile but congenial. The relations belong to us and we to them. Understanding a context or even a whole network of contexts is vitally necessary. It is not an intellectual luxury but an absolutely essential action.

How far are these contexts really present on their own, how far are they not first generated by interpretations that do not need exposition but apply to each fresh instance the prejudgments of a science or a preexistent opinion concerning humanity? Can we trust those concerned to read themselves so plainly that they elucidate and justify the theoretical conjectures that are applied to them? The Wolf-Man speaks in somewhat Sibylline fashion of the new world that is opened up for him by analysis. Is it simply the world that he did not know before, that was previously obscure to him, and that has now become clear so that he can begin to live a life of relationships in it? Or is it a new world of better explanations of existence, the partially organized world that Nietzsche in his own way also had in view? Such counterquestions are not new but have to be kept in mind in any exposition and also in literary interpretation, which is always in danger of reading into a text what we want to read out of it. No text is safe against being used as a quarry for building our own world. For our theme the problem of exposition is especially relevant because the question of meaning that derives meanings from contexts is a kind of final issue. We cannot get behind it. Only with its help can we probe more deeply into the normally hidden contextual conditions of existence and explore fully their unsearchable wealth of relations. Every text, whether biographical or written, points to another text. Constant cross-references give the impression of a solid totality in which we can move. Even if we survey only one part of this totality, it is supported by the confidence that every element in it is related to a countless number of others. Here again we have confirmation of something we have noted time and again, namely, that when we ask about meaning we do not fall out of the world.

What I mean by saying that the question of meaning is the final issue I will elucidate by means of the other forms of its application that Nietzsche's criticism of the meaning of suffering has also evoked. Mischances, sicknesses, and other serious disruptions of the normal course become occasions to inquire into reasons for the misfortune with a view to reconciling ourselves to its consequences. Those who know why they suffer will suffer no less, but their pain at the riddle of suffering can be mitigated. Those who find the reason in experience move into a context that enables them perhaps to solve their puzzle. If possible they will even succeed in appropriating the reasons in such a way that they become part of their attitude and invulnerability results. This was the counsel of Job's friends when they traced back every misfortune to some failing. "Think now, who that was innocent ever perished?" (4:7). Then Zophar: "If you direct your heart rightly, you will stretch out your hands toward him. If iniquity is in your hand, put it far away, and do not let wickedness dwell in your tents. Surely then you will lift up your face without blemish, you will be secure, and will not fear" (11:13-15). As I shall have to show later, Job found no comfort in these recommendations. Indeed, he vehemently refused to commit himself to contexts that would have deflected him from God in favor of relations in which, according to the view of his friends, God's rule would be restricted by observable effects.

The admonitions of these pious sages that we should be content to relate right conduct to well-being and fear of God to blessing, and not to look beyond these in invocation of God, are an abiding prototype of explanations of existence that trace back suffering to guilt and refusal and declare it to be divinely justified. The form of such interpretations has changed. Other more conclusive relations and illuminating deductions have been introduced. Guilt has been sought less in one's own deeds and more in those of others or in relationships. But their character has remained the same. Meaning is ascertained and found in connections that light up what is darkly incomprehensible and show that

suffering is not totally devoid of reference. The other trend in psychotherapy that does not view the meaning of relationship in terms of
analytical exposition stresses the danger of losing oneself in explanations
and not accepting responsibility for oneself in the here and now. On
this view meaning discloses itself in the intensity with which we throw
ourselves into life with our whole existence and without retrospective
unveiling by others. Meaning is experienced, we are told, only by those
who rely on their immediate experience of reality, an experience that
cannot be attained to or conceived of at all by action but that lies at the
basis of everything.

One who knows how to depict such experience, the psychiatrist
Hans C. Syz, tells in some notes from his student days (1916) of an
experience in which all perceptions and thought connections dissolved:
"The great anxiety I now feel seems, I think, to be due to the fact that
a great nothing is now suddenly found to be the basis of personality,
that the human soul is simply made up of feelings and thought-forms,
and that what I sought further in it is not there."[23] But this nothing
yielded to a new being that manifested itself in the depth of its own
vitality: "We do not go, we are carried; this was what I experienced
directly."[24] What is experienced is the basis of life that communicates
itself through the dynamic core of the person and also links this self
incomprehensibly to life outside its consciousness. "The meaning of life
does not lie outside us but in us. It lies in life itself. It consists of living
life in general."[25] All states of consciousness, thoughts, external relations,
and links to others, in short, all the things that are seen as reality, express
this dynamic. Being, which properly exists only in ourselves, is sustained
outwardly.[26] In this tireless movement it finds support in the cosmic life
from which every authentic expression of existence comes and to which
it returns.

I might go on to say that this experience finds illustration in its
pathological antitheses, in the experience of a vacuum, a lack of feeling
for the self, a hopeless self-emptying such as we find with innumerable
variations in psychotherapeutic writings. There are so many complaints

23. H. C. Syz, *Vom Sein und vom Sinn* (Zurich, 1972), 8f.
24. Ibid., 19.
25. Ibid., 36.
26. Ibid., 12.

of the impression of basic loss, of being drained of all vital forces, and of resultant tedium or indefinite anxiety, that the picture of sickness seems to be well established. Lack of meaning is diagnosed, and since meaning gives security, confidence, and orientation of the will to live, it seems that in view of the causes of sickness we must ask who in earlier times, when practically no one asked about meaning in this sense, managed to get along without asking. Then it is no great step to the conclusion that the great sources of confidence in past times were moral values, universally binding goals in an intact society, institutions that gave meaning such as church and state or the legal and educational systems. All these were then secure, and above all God was accepted without question as the ground of meaning and being.

Such explanations, however, still leave out the decisive question what this meaning really is, the lack of which lets us infer possibilities for healing. Is it just a singular linguistic phenomenon that people did not speak about meaning earlier as they do today? The question of meaning gives evidence of no lack of meaning whose background can be satisfactorily explained in terms of social history or psychology as a process of disintegration that compels us to seek and find meaning. Might not the very opposite be argued, namely, that the urge to find meaning is itself a disintegrating and destructive factor? What has actually changed in society and in the constitution of the psyche can be due to ultimate attitudes for which a social majority has decided for inner reasons and to which we owe both the normal concept of a healthy life and the corresponding picture of sickness. There is only one way to test this conjecture and to find out how far it is true, namely, to see what has self-evidently taken place, or what it means to be oriented to meaning without question.

Therapists who prescribe meaning as an elixir agree that we all need a fixed reference point by which to orient what we either do or do not do. The unchanging factor in the ocean of relativities, the final resting place without which none of us can manage, is called meaning. It sets us in fruitful tension with our usual conduct and with what have become the outward circumstances of life. All healthy people, it is assumed, will constantly be in tension between meaning and existence. In their real selves they are always ahead of themselves. This tension can be exploited therapeutically. With its help new courage for life can be created and more surely directed.

Meaning itself, however, is surprisingly imprecise. Necessarily so, we must now say, for precise meaning would not be the ultimate resting place and constant reference point because it could not be the source of all determinations. A definite meaning would be one meaning among others and therefore relative again. We would have to put to it the counterquestion, but how could we when beyond meaning we can experience nothing that sustains and secures us? Hence we can never give meaning a name. That we are referred to it totally is shown by our receiving it in relations. Buber wanted to make this point when he spoke of the sense of relation that takes up everything into itself in such a way that it moves toward what is other than itself and is grounded in mutuality. We receive, and we do not receive content but a presence, a presence as a force.[27] This force upholds the relations in and by which we live. But it is also powerful enough to change everything that encounters us into relations.

Here again we see the reversal that occupied Nietzsche greatly as the birth of the question of meaning. Our values are interpreted as things. Is there then meaning merely in being? Is not meaning necessarily the sense and perspective of relation? All meaning is the will for power; all the meaning of relationship comes down to this.[28] The chorus of meaning-therapists naturally protested strongly against the reduction of meaning to the will for power, and thought it may be asked whether the protest was an honest one in view of the sublimation of the will for power as a will for self-mastery and self-redemption. But apart from that, Nietzsche also expresses exactly that which has come to be known as the primal experience of meaning, namely, that of the relativity of all phenomena and even of all values to the sense of relation that is set forth in the meaning of relationship. The later Nietzsche certainly views all experience from the standpoint of its center in the interpreting subject as the basis of all reality, not in being itself. Yet even the commitment to meaning does not save us from experiencing our own personal being in the full sense of the self as the center of every angle from which we approach meaning.

We find here an elective affinity between confidence in a sense of relation and the religious sense. Those who discovered the religious

27. *I and Thou.*
28. F. Nietzsche, *Aus dem Nachlass der Achtzigerjahre,* in *Werke,* III, 503.

sense had gone beyond the confines of thought and action, neither of which attains to that which is primal: thought because it does not originally produce anything but can only reflect on what is there; action because it aims more at something specific and achieves it, but loses sight of the totality. Feeling alone passes over these limits because it expresses its absolute debt to everything that communicates itself to it. In the light of these distinctions we can look at all things and understand them in terms of their origin. By studying the history of the development of the religious sense we can see how it interprets all the given factors of the Christian faith such as the Bible, church, and confession, along with the institutions of other religions, as forms of expression for piety, and how it appropriates them to expound itself. The Bible and confession, of course, are also respected as expressions of the feelings of their authors, but only to the degree that they kindle religious feeling today or at least permit it to rediscover itself in the tradition. We can take traditions seriously along these lines, protect them against blind repudiation, and continue them, yet only as they understand themselves, undergo new development, and let themselves be carried forward in interpretations. This process of dissolution and reconstruction is veiled when we ask what is the meaning of all these things, what is their significance for religious feeling, and what is their final content that expresses itself in piety and relates the pious to the *universum*. The transforming into meaning and relationships of meaning is accompanied by an ambiguity in the terms that like a kaleidoscope permits new combinations between meaning and basic content, relation, receptivity, and structuring.

The religious sense abandons the position of faith, which is conditioned by hearing the Word of God that judges and saves. It also leaves the community of faith in order to forge new links out of a spirit of piety, and then, enriched in this way, to join the church again or to attach itself to a new religious association. The summons to final meaning or to the meaning of life equips us for similar discoveries. Those who obey it and seek this meaning are no longer tied for better or for worse to their situation. The resolute step toward meaning is the decisive thing even though it does not lead directly ahead, as outward aims and goals do, but remains a step toward what is fundamental. Here again individuals are to see their relations to others and to things, to tasks and to values, as under their own control so that they may make their own choices. Brought under the denominator of meaning, all things involve the giving of meaning. Only thus are they understandable and only thus can they help to establish the sense of what is new that sees life as worth living. As regards social relationships, we have to inquire into the meaning that they already have in order to construct and to make effective fulfilled relations. They no longer serve merely as reference points for sensory experience and action. Those who track down their meaning interpret them from a wealth of angles. This is, however, a transitory process in which the interpreters (all of us!) expound themselves because they will find no meaning otherwise. Insight into social relations is not so much an encouragement to learn to live in them as a spur to the finding and positing of demands for meaning in them, and therefore to their exploitation for the free construction of possible relationships and the structuring of a meaningful life.

Recommendations of this sort may be found in all fields of human endeavor, not only in psychotherapy but also in ethics,[29] in religious education,[30] and in pastoral care, an important factor in the need to

29. H. Ringeling, *Ethik vor der Sinnfrage: Religiöse Aspekte der Verantwortung* (Gütersloh, 1982), 9: "The anthropological situation is at root a religious situation that is open to a Christian communication of meaning to life, a theological interpretation of reality." On the question of meaning as a religious exposition of the basics of action cf. M. Honecker, *Bildung in der Sinnkrise unserer Gesellschaft* (1977); idem, *Perspektiven christlicher Gesellschaftsdeutung* (Gütersloh, 1981), 128ff., esp. 138ff. Also connected with the question of meaning in ethics is a turning to personal worth and the individual question of the basis and goal of life over against all overriding and supposedly all-controlling sociopolitical goals that rule out such a question, as in Marxist humanism. Cf. M. Machovec, *Vom Sinn des menschlichen Lebens* (Freiburg, 1971) (in Czech: Prague, 1965); H. F. Steiner, *Marxisten-Leninisten über den Sinn des Lebens* (Essen, 1970); H. Rolfes, *Der Sinn des Lebens im marxistischen Denken* (Düsseldorf, 1971). But even at the far pole from this kind of thinking we can read in K. R. Popper that the meaning of life is not something hidden that we can find in life but something that we ourselves can give to life. By what we do and do not do, by our work and influence, by our attitude to life and others and the world, we can make life meaningful (*Selbstbefreiung durch das Wissen: Der Sinn der Geschichte*, ed. L. Reinisch, 5th ed. (Munich, 1974), 102.

30. In this regard Tillich's thinking in particular has found acceptance, and not only among Protestants; cf. H. Halbfas, *Theory of Catechetics: Language and Experience in Religious Education* (ET New York, 1971), 18-19. The question of meaning in religious education has now tended to merge into the search for personal identity and community-building goals. Religious traditions are seen along such lines and integrated into the various interpretations of meaning; cf. Halbfas, *Aufklärung und Widerstand* (Stutt-

integrate the question of meaning being that such spheres often overlap. As an example among many we read in Frankl that today's meaning is tomorrow's value. The meaning that an alert conscience finds may well become a universal and universally binding value. That is perhaps the way in which religions and revolutions arise.[31] All that may well happen in a society that has only more immediate goals and no binding norms. As universals of meaning,[32] values then take on new significance. Ethics, however, decays when it is traced back to the discovery of meaning that is supposed to help those who act find their identity — an identity that we achieve only by self-fulfillment. The ominous basic value of self-fulfillment is typical of the linguistic confusion that has set in with the question of meaning. If self-fulfillment means authentic existence, the full and indivisible self in responsible action, this is no less self-evident anthropologically than it is fateful as an ethical and therapeutical maxim. When elevated into the goal of action, self-fulfillment has to have a limiting sense, since others come into consideration only insofar as they confirm or disrupt. In the name of self-fulfillment we may develop a supreme sense of responsibility, but we are not really referred in the process to anyone or to anything else. The whole world in all its variety is seen and handled from the standpoint of the core of the person. Meaning as it were confers a plenary sense of the self, which need be concerned about nothing whatever in the world since ultimately and most profoundly it is in harmony with the world.

What may we really ascertain from all this? The religious sense that prepared the ground for confidence in the meaning of relation was trying to address the real world. It hoped to overcome the sensory deceptions underlying all physical perceptions. In addition to facing this danger it also wanted to check the destructive division of the world, to make it one that we can understand and control. Its concern was for the higher unity of reality and humanity that the cleft between rationality and activity threatened. It thus went a step back behind both of

---

gart and Düsseldorf, 1971), 18 and 106; K. E. Nipkow, *Grunkfragen der Religionspädagogik,* vol. I (Gütersloh, 1975), 140. In criticism of this trend cf. G. Ringshausen, "Erfahrung und Sinnfrage als Horizont des Religionsunterrichtes," *Der evangelische Erzieher* 34 (1982), 203ff. (with bibliography).

31. Frankl, *Aphoristische Bemerkungen,* 425n.11.
32. Ibid., 425.

these and in feeling sought direct access to meaningful reality, that is, reality filled with meaning. The question of meaning that took this path thus became the question of human beings themselves, their unity and totality. The question of the meaning of life was raised because human life threatens to become externalized and alienated under the promises of reflection and work. This concern, however, was not on account of sensory experiences and actions, which are dubious for cogent reasons. It is a radical concern vis-à-vis the absolute antithesis of meaning and meaninglessness, of being and nonbeing under which it sees all the achievements of life placed. Nietzsche described it as a defensive measure that is vitally necessary. As he put it, we share with animals the sense of truth that is basically the same as the sense of security. We are not prepared to deceive ourselves or to be led astray by ourselves. We do not trust what our passions tell us. We restrain ourselves and are constantly on the watch against ourselves. Animals understand this as well as we do. In them, too, self-control develops out of a sense of the real (out of shrewdness).[33]

This comparison offends, perhaps, our human dignity, for our sense of the true world seems to rise above any mere securing of our existence. But does not our concern for the meaning of life show that the supposed distinction is deceptive? Does not the effort to keep the self intact and not let it disintegrate show itself to be an act of integration that simply wants to maintain in being a life that is under constant threat? The sense of truth, then, sees only the antithesis of meaning and meaninglessness, and it relates all that it perceives to this antithesis. It thus sees the whole field of perceptions as a matter of perspectives; it cannot be concerned only about limited objective meaning. The whole world is, as it were, on its heart. Without its input this world would fall to pieces. It can find no place for the objective meaning that does not stand in the same way, or at all, under the question of being or nonbeing.

Making everything a matter of perspectives, however, destroys perception, which is a matter of proportions. Should not the religious sense, in treading the frontiers, have come across proportions of this kind, not the infinite superiority of the world of spirit over that of sense but the fact that we run up against our corporeality, which also limits our feelings? Our limited time between birth and death is similarly one of

33. Nietzsche, *Morgenröte*, in *Werke*, I, 1031f.

the basics within which created existence moves and which can never be brought into experience. The otherness of all other people is another immovable limit to all experience. Does not the understanding of given factors such as these have to be taken into account, too? Reflections on sense and meaning in all their nuances does indeed regard understanding as among the achievements that control not merely sense perceptions but also themselves. But the decisive question prior to that of meaning is precisely this: Does understanding owe itself to truth? Truth here cannot be a clothing of human self-securing in distinction from self-deception. It opposes falsehood, which does not simply hold to a mistake but cannot accept the truth. Temporality, corporeality, otherness, and understanding are proportions, that is, specific relations that are there between us and what is already present for us before all reflection and outside all action.

One test of this, if not the decisive one, is how we perceive suffering, for pain at suffering cannot be conceived of simply in terms of the genealogy of the question of meaning. Even today when we ask about meaning, along with the meaning of life and work, we ask especially about the meaning of suffering in all its forms. Suffering seems indeed to be the origin of understanding. Those who suffer do not merely inquire into the why and wherefore of the suffering that has overtaken them but into the meaning of a life that cannot avoid misfortune, sickness, and death in spite of all our safeguards against them. Suffering obviously brings to light the question of meaning that is always there though mostly concealed. If we can supply the meaning of suffering, life with all its incomprehensible adversities is justified. It is not enough, of course, merely to define a specific form of suffering in antithesis to health or prosperity. That would not deal with suffering in itself but only with some specific suffering in its relation to life and death, and as in Ecclesiastes we might then be led to the recognition that it has its time and that in some hidden relation to God's action this is the right time that unexpectedly enables us to give thanks for it.

Such ideas are strange and even hostile, however, to the question of the meaning of suffering. This question does indeed reflect on the fact that suffering is part of life. But for this reason all suffering can and must be a provocation for life, whether as a challenge to alleviate the suffering so far as possible and thus conceivably to lessen its threat to life, or as a spur to the restoration of health by mending the broken relations either from within or without, or by an integrating of the suffering into life that enables us to live with it and to be healthy in that way. Suffering in the sense of a comprehensive question of meaning that requires explanation is an interruption of normal relations. It demands that the gap that has opened up be closed again in some lasting way. It thus becomes an occasion for the establishing of individual or social meaning.

To ask about the meaning of suffering is not to submit to it but to accept it as one accepts a challenge. Suffering as a challenge to life[34] implies resistance that cannot avoid recognition of suffering because pain, loneliness, anxiety, and death cannot for the moment be totally banished from the world. Even though they are unavoidable, however, we are told that no one should simply give way to them. If they reduce us to silence and do not let us look beyond them, where results speak for them, life is for us truly at an end. Thus the question of the meaning of suffering is a salutary one, for it tries to rescue those who suffer from the meaninglessness that has fallen upon them. Suffering would destroy us if we could not ask what it means, if we could not resist it, if we could not be induced to take up arms against the naked and definitive facticity of suffering.

Inquiry into the meaning of suffering along these lines means seeing it as an interruption, a rift, or even a deep cleft in the relations of life and the context of existence. Meaning then becomes the bridge that we can cross over, the possibility of continuing on our way even if by some other track. The higher value of meaning, its fruitful distinction from meaning in the ordinary sense, becomes particularly clear, it seems, in relation to suffering. The circumstances of suffering are thus treated as a text that is a key to life with all its weaknesses and strengths, all its promises and dangers. Sufferings are significant as pointers to crises of a vital, personal, or social nature. They summon both those who suffer and those who aid them to restore the shattered relationship of meaning

---

34. H. Wiersinga, *Leid: Herausforderungen des Lebens: Auseinandersetzung mit einer Grundfrage* (Munich, 1982) (in Dutch: Baarn, 1975); M. Kessel, "Der Arzt vor der Frage nach Wesen und Sinn der Krankheit," *Jubiläumsheft zum 50 jährigen Bestehen der Berliner Arbeitsgemeinschaft Arzt und Seelsorger, Berliner Hefte für Evangelische Krankenseelsorge* 37 (Berlin, 1975), 37f.: "Medically sickness is always and in all cases meaningless. Meaning can be found only in a total context in which health and sickness are related as two alternative manifestations of life."

or to reconstruct it.[35] Cries of distress are always signs of life, and the fact that they expect an answer is an indication, however slight, that meaning is also present as a communication link. For this reason advocates of the question of meaning find they can heal, or at least help, by establishing relations with those who suffer and can assist them by letting them know that they are no longer devoid of such relations.

The question of meaning seeks to create space when action has run up against a barrier that it cannot overcome. Those who cannot defeat it but begin to experience the pain of suffering set themselves a new goal with the question and in this way find a space between possible answers and the painful self-experience. Their intentions are now directed from within because they can no longer work outward. They ask what it is to be truly human in an extreme situation, but the answer is guided by the desire to interpret and mold that represents the bearer of meaning with its product. Those who suffer are active creatively, though naturally in a space that they have measured out for themselves and will now traverse.

A space of this kind is created by the question of the basis and goal of life. The question itself seems already to be a step beyond the immutability of suffering, a first step toward deliverance from mere suffering. It thus differs from a diagnosing of meaningful elements in suffering. Who is content merely to experience what suffering is and what it is from which one suffers? References to causes do not give any further help if they do not explain why and to what end the misfortune has come upon one. The question of suffering is an attempt to learn more, to know why one has to suffer. I have already sketched an answer given by the Judeo-Christian tradition, that is, suffering as the consequence of a failing, an indication of one's own guilt or that of others. Another classical solution that is repeatedly mentioned is the awakening of the religious sense, namely, that God uses suffering to move people to reflection, penitence, and conversion from the sham world of perverted goals in life. Today, however, these two answers are mostly referred to only to show by means of them that while they may help sufferers to

---

35. Cf. M. Josuttis, "Der Sinn der Krankheit, Ergebung oder Protest?" *Praxis des Evangeliums zwischen Politik und Religion: Grundprobleme der praktischen Theologie* (Munich, 1974), 117ff.; idem, "Der Seelsorger vor die Frage nach dem Sinn der Krankheit," in *Vom Wesen und Sinn der Krankheit,* 19ff.

self-examination and to the accepting of their destiny from the hands
of God, they are unable to motivate sufferers to enter into their suffering
and to receive from it a forward prod. For they do not give meaning to
suffering, an understanding that suffering does not have to be final, that
God will overcome it, and that it can thus be removed, even if by ever
so small steps, also in the process of the maturation of sufferers, of their
integrating of contrary experiences, and of inner enrichment by the
experience of possibilities of life not hitherto envisioned.[36] Sufferers
find meaning when they understand that this is not the end for them
even though, at least for the time, they can do no more. Suffering
appears here as a crisis of the will to live. Whether it is a power to save
depends on whether, either as those who suffer or those who do not for
the moment suffer, we will accept it as a challenge to live life to the full.

But what if suffering means the end not only of action but of
reflection on its meaning? What if it is so intense that those who suffer
cannot even measure the objective significance of their destiny because
for the moment they cannot even think of its opposite? All thinking
and feeling are gathered up in pain. Others may do something for the
sufferers, but they cannot take from them the fact that suffering has
come upon them specifically, and they cannot help them by vicariously
thinking for them and communicating to them a meaning that is not
theirs.

In suffering unveiled humanity is perceived precisely when all interpretations fail and the time of action, even of the action that gives
meaning, has ended. Suffering, I perceive what I do not want to perceive.
Decisive now is whether I seek to escape this situation, perhaps by saying

---

36. H. C. Piper, *Krankheit — Erleben und Lernen* (Munich, 1974), 30ff.; Wiersinga,
Leid, 131ff.; with reservations Wintzer, "Sinn und Erfahrung," 222ff. What has changed
relative to the theological tradition may be seen strikingly from the Melanchthon quotation in Piper, *Krankheit*, 30 (and cf. his "Vom Sinn des Leidens," *Pastoraltheologie* 56
[1967], 503). Piper's rendering is that we can tolerate nothing that does not have some
meaning. Cf. Melanchthon's 1559 *Loci*, in *Werke*, II/2, ed. H. Engelland (Gütersloh,
1953), 635. Melanchthon's real point is that we cannot love or accept anything unless
we can count on something good in it, namely, the goodness of God. What protects us
against doubt is not just meaning but the saving will of God. Because God slays and
makes alive, misfortune, too, drives us into his arms. We are not splitting theological
hairs if we see a difference here from the religious conviction that nothing is without
meaning.

what God does not will, in which case suffering is already overcome inwardly, or perhaps by saying that I will nothing more, in which case again I have the suffering behind me, having submitted and reconciled myself to it; only if I say neither, however, is justice done to God. In suffering human self-will and the living God confront one another. God takes the place of human self-will, but without eliminating the human person, without this person willing to will no more. Paul had this in mind when he said that God had denied his request for personal strength and given him the comfort that God's strength is made perfect in weakness (2 Cor. 12:9). God does not reveal himself as the Almighty in suffering. He enters into our human weakness and takes it upon himself. Suffering points us to a life that is defined by the presence of God. "It is no longer I who live, but Christ who lives in me. And the life I now live in the flesh I live by faith in the Son of God, who loved me and gave himself for me" (Gal. 2:20). What suffering gives, then, is not space but patience, not surrender but steadfastness, which endures the tension between nonwilling and the will of God, and which lets God's work take place, not foreseeing how.

The perception of the creative opposition of God to human self-will might be called the discovery of meaning. But that would be a play on words that conceals the profound antithesis to the interpretive giving of meaning that seeks to help sufferers not to fall out of the world. Nietzsche observed that we cannot tolerate meaninglessness, the merciless "I do not know why." We project and establish meaning in order to live. All the senses must subject themselves to this higher sense without being able to be conscious of their mistakes. For this sense imparts a creative illusion to the meaningless world and therefore everything that serves self-preservation is right for it. We can no longer question the giving of meaning because it makes known to us nothing beyond itself. Within it we can only try to avoid false conclusions that threaten life. For this reason Nietzsche offered the slogan: Back from sense to the senses! Insofar as the senses show us becoming, perishing, and changing, they do not lie.[37] Beyond that there is nothing to perceive. Everything depends on our not going under in the becoming and perishing.

Even if we do not accept that slogan, the question of meaning that

37. Nietzsche, *Twilight of the Idols* (Penguin ed., London, 1961), 37.

puts the idea of a universe of relationships of meaning in place of perception of our humanity is highly questionable. Even if with a different intention than Nietzsche's liberation of the world and humanity *from* responsibility in God[38] and *for* human self-responsibility, it is an element of anticipated redemption. How talk about God confronts it and disputes its right to be a final resting place, and how faith, as a new sense, contradicts the religious sense, we must now investigate.

38. Ibid., 54. "We deny God, we deny responsibility in God; only in that way do we redeem the world."

VII. SCRIPTURE AND MEANING

T HE FALSE paths and dead ends that Nietzsche found in the labyrinth of sense and meaning are not strange to Christianity when it considers its own history. Experience of them should warn theology and the church today not to take up the question of meaning blindly. Nietzsche hit upon an exposed nerve when he expounded the origin of the question in terms of pain at suffering and the Christian vice of not accepting life as it is. Christians (and not just theologians) as Nietzsche defined them are born interpreters. They understand themselves only when they have expounded themselves as existent and reduced life to speech in such a way that it promises them a goal — the apparently fruitful self-deception of an artificial sense that despises and stunts our natural human senses.

In Christianity (and Judaism), however, exposition and interpretation go back to the question of meaning in another way as well. In theological tradition sense *(sensus)* is used for the sense of Holy Scripture. This sense is not restricted to the meaning of individual words and phrases that are handed down authoritatively and that must be known exactly and without deviation if we are to remain traditionally orthodox. Sense primarily means what God himself has told us about himself: God's Word as the beginning of all human perception of God and his world. It denotes the presence of the Holy Spirit for us. As God's it evades all human concepts and prior knowledge, yet it also makes God's ways known in such a way that we can speak of them and follow them. "Who has directed [or

101

'measured,' as we might also render it] the Spirit of the Lord?" That is the prophet's question when he looks at the immeasurable creative power of God (Isa. 40:13), having previously depicted the Spirit of God as a hot wind that causes all our seemingly blossoming life of human constructs to wither and fade (v. 7). Paul takes up the question after vainly trying to fathom God's judgment on his people and his promise to the race (Rom. 11:34). The Latin Bible has *sensus* here, and Luther used *Sinn* in the sense of "mind," which is the NRSV rendering: "Who has known the mind of the Lord?" But what is totally concealed in God is so far manifest that we may direct ourselves by it and trust its leading. To understand the sense of Scripture is to know how to speak with God and not to want to go back behind his Word.

The question of the sense or meaning of Scripture acquired its profile, however, only after the fixing of the canon, the drawing of the safe and necessary boundary by means of which the early church differentiated the sacred Scriptures from all the other traditions of pious experience and theological insight. With its decision regarding the canon the church confessed the definitiveness of God's revelation. This confession was and is sustained by confidence that the truth imparted in Scripture embraces the church's present and future. In the sense of the biblical text was enclosed openness to knowledge of God's coming into history. Hence there is no need of future or ongoing revelation or of constant unfolding of the revelation that took place and that is handed down. Hermeneutics here is simply the establishing of this sense of Scripture. It is not bound up, as later, with the problem of putting a tradition in terms of the present life of the interpreter.

The theological meaning of Scripture is established (not fixed!) when with the help of the exposition of a text God's action can be expected on good grounds. But already in the first deliberations of early biblical exposition this simple task of understanding ran up against a twofold danger. For one thing it was thought that we can honor the dignity of the Bible only if each text can be shown to be meaningful for faith. Because God imparts himself totally in Scripture, all of it gives direction for faith, and it is thus to be expounded in this sense in each of its ever so tiny details. We must pass on the meaning by biblical references of all kinds. We must see in every ordinary circumstance or simple report a divine communication that has significance for the lives of all of us at all times. As the sixteenth century passed into the seven-

teenth, the Reformed theologian Benedictus Aretius inquired along
these lines into the sense *(sensus)* of the biblical histories, which have,
of course, a surface meaning but also offer us a sense that binds our
senses to Christ.[1] An extreme illustration is the eugenic experiment of
Jacob, who by means of it secured the redemption of the promise of
blessing (Gen. 30:37ff.). What took place here did not in fact bear a
Christian sense, but spiritual interpretation can give this! That this art
of interpreting robs the story of its true significance in biblical theology
was not considered.

The other danger was that the reality with which faith has to do
was felt to be increasingly complex and varied. First faith is set in history
that is narrated, and has to be narrated again and again, and therefore
it must pay attention to what has been reported as having taken place
(the word *historia* has in this older expository tradition, and well on
into the Middle Ages, the sense of a story that is told, also in the plural,
not the modern sense of a sequence of events).[2] I have already sketched
a second dimension of the understanding of faith. In addition to its so
to speak obvious meaning each event has a background meaning that
relates it to God and his action. Against the background of this spiritual
sense the reality as it is known only from its external structure seems
incomplete and even pitiful. Only in the light of the sense filled out by
God's rule can it be viewed in all its riches. Third, I must also mention
the action that needs direction to take the right path, and each text that
is binding for faith must offer something along these lines. Finally, the
hope of faith needs specific orientation in order to be able to see the
present in the light of him who is to come and to distinguish the future
from all human prospects. No history of and with God can become the
past if God has declared himself in it in some other way. By directing
our gaze upon God each history has significance as a pointer to the
future because it kindles expectation of God and sees already in what
has taken place a first glimpse of what is still to come.

Out of this bunch of views the theory of the fourfold sense of

1. Benedictus Aretius, *S. S. theologiae problemata, h.e. loci communes Christianae
religionis methodice explicati, a Locus I, II: De allegoriis* (Geneva, 1617), 283.

2. Along these lines Aretius refers to the sense of a history. If this yields only
something insipid and crude, then the mystical sense better expounds natural things
(causes) and an allegorical interpretation is preferable.

Scripture developed.[3] This theory aimed to give as much weight to the inner integrating of reality as to the different forms of human perception. It believed that we can be totally human before God only in the unity of recollection and expectation, hope and love, body and spirit, the outward and the inward. Sometimes there was a linked to it what is almost a theory of ecclesiastical sociology that does not view the whole person individually, or seldom does so, but usually sees the whole person actualized only in the body of the church as a totality. The building up of the fellowship of faith is referred to a hierarchy of interpreters of whom only the upper echelon can penetrate to the true depths of the text. Simple believers cannot take in the full sense of a biblical text. Most of them must rely on the ethical instructions that others derive from the Bible. To perceive the presence of God they must go to the church's means of grace. They must be content to know that they belong to this church.

Martin Luther's criticism of the fourfold sense is perfectly understandable when we pay sufficient heed to its double thrust: first, against the total imaging of God's saving work in a multiple reality; and second, against its social manifestation. Luther, then, demanded that all of us should be able both to read the Bible and to understand it. This understanding would be oriented solely to God's work toward us, which is not the goal of a hermeneutical task but itself takes place in the work of the gospel. For Luther the basic hermeneutical principle was that the sense of any biblical text is what promotes Christ.[4] The exposition of any biblical saying can do only one thing, that is, clear away, so far as is humanly possible, the obstacles that block us from seeing God's working. To get at the sense of the biblical text is to let God work.

The Reformation exposition of Scripture resolutely contested the notion that the Bible has any other purpose than to mediate the work of God or that it can be understood in any other way than as God's active Word. Luther and the other reformers agreed with the Humanist

3. On what follows cf. H. de Lubac, *Les quatre sens de l'Écriture*, I, II, 2 (Paris, 1959), 64; G. Ebeling, *Evangelische Evangelienauslegung: Eine Untersuchung zu Luthers Hermeneutik* (1942; repr. Darmstadt, 1962); W. Raddatz, G. Sauter, and H. G. Ulrich, "Verstehen," *Praktisch-Theologisches Handbuch*, ed. G. Otto, 2nd ed. (Hamburg, 1975), 622, line 33.

4. Cf. Luther's preface to James and Jude (1522), in which he argues that all proper sacred books preach and promote Christ (WA, VII, 58; LW, 35, 395).

reformers of the day that each biblical text must be expounded grammatically, that is, with linguistic accuracy. But this insistence on the natural sense sought to set aside all pious and less pious preconceptions. In no case should the Bible be read as a mere history book or collection of edifying illustrations with a view to better conduct. It is not enough, stressed Luther, nor is it Christian, to proclaim Christ's works, life, and words purely historically, as though they were ordinary events that we need to know only as examples of the right way to live.[5] What is written in the Bible is said "for us," as Luther especially constantly insisted. In the first instance "for us" here means that each biblical saying is directed at us as the verdict of God that judges and saves. God's Word always strikes us in a specific way: as the law with which God demands his rights, and as the gospel which pardons the ungodly and promises them salvation. Law and gospel are not literary categories. The Bible cannot be divided into two groups of texts. Each text seeks to be heard as both law and gospel how and when God wills. It is not to be read in either the one way or the other, for then we would know the sense in advance and would take it out of the text. Understood as God's Word, the Bible itself gives us the sense, but not always the same sense or the same sense to each person at the same time. Nor does the double nature of God's Word mean that there is a sequence in which God reduces us to despair by terrifying demands and thus drives us into his arms in order that we may be able to hear the saving Word of the gospel. That God's Word encounters us as law or gospel is not a principle of understanding but a criterion for our understanding. God's Word is God's speaking to us, his verdict of death or life for us. We cannot get behind this. We cannot think about God without speaking about him in this way in which he has spoken and speaks to us. We are prevented from pushing through to God himself and then, familiar with him, trying to say what only he himself can say.

Even in the Protestant understanding of Scripture this revision of the question of the sense of the biblical text has not always been grasped accurately or clearly enough. There was a natural temptation to make of the theological principle of God's action "for us" a new common denominator for a supposedly better and more helpful understanding of the Bible, for example, by interpreting the whole Bible in its saving

5. Cf. Luther, *On the Freedom of a Christian* (1520), WA, VII, 58; LW, 31, 357.

sense as a message of salvation, reconciliation, or liberation, or by seeing
in it a saving speech event that rescues us from being closed in upon
ourselves and hence creates salutary living relations.[6] But a general sense
of this kind does not let the Bible speak. The Bible has to be received
by faith. Faith cannot be a precondition for understanding. It is part of
the working of the divine Word. It is perception of God's action, a
perception that God himself brings into being in order that we who are
"curved in upon ourselves" may receive the truth about God and ourselves.

In this way faith becomes aware that Christ has intervened for us
and that he gives us participation in eternal life in fellowship with God.
This act on our behalf, quite apart from all historical approaches, means
that the Bible was written for us and is addressed to us.[7] The Bible
speaks of the absolute beginning with God's act. Therein lies its *sensus*.
It is for this reason that theological questions about meaning are referred
to the meaning of Scripture, not because Christianity is a book religion
which in distinction from other religions has to do primarily with
textual manifestations of the divine revelation.

This was why Luther put theological understanding under the theological rule of the doctrine of justification. God calls us out of the
ungodly way in which we are closed in upon ourselves, out of our effort
to base our existence on achievement and to set life as a goal that we
can reach in seeking after God. Even the relationships of life that we
regard as meaningful, in which we establish ourselves, and into which
we integrate whatever encounters us — though they may well have to
be twisted and falsified to do this — even these are expressions of this
need for justification. As God by his verdict asserts his own rights to
human beings and the world, he breaks not only all our human arro-
gance but also the intellectual attempt to achieve security in the world,
especially by the contexts of meaning that we have constructed and to

6. Cf. G. Ebeling, "The Word of God and Hermeneutics," in *Word and Faith* (ET
Philadelphia, 1963), 325-26, on the distinction between God's Word and the human
word in the Bible, which relates to whether the word event is misused and corrupted
by us or whether it is holy and pure and fulfilled, i.e., what it ought to be as it is intended,
and as we naturally see it in human relations according to this intention.

7. Luther's Theses on Faith no. 24 at the disputation on 9.11.1535, WA, XXXIX/1,
46: "For this 'for me' or 'for us' effects true faith and distinguishes it from all other belief
that simply accepts facts."

which we have accustomed ourselves. We are told by God's verdict who we are, who we can be, and where we are heading, namely, to the fulfillment of our lives in fellowship with God. Hence the need for justification is silenced once and for all. We now receive our reality, like that of the world, only from this verdict, not as a product of our own achievement, no matter what the appearance of this may be.

It is possible, then, to measure objective meaning by this verdict. As the apostle Paul says: "Be transformed by the renewing of your minds, that you may discern what is the will of God — what is good and acceptable and perfect" (Rom. 12:2). Justification is not this transforming of the mind, but it manifests itself in it. If the mind, the organ of testing and distinguishing, is not transformed, attention to the meaning of the text will soon be twisted again into the interpreting that seizes on some content from the Bible — it might even be the doctrine of justification — in order to make this "sense" the key to the exposition of individual biblical texts and to exploit it on behalf of everything that comes within the purview of the pious mind. The understanding of the Bible, then, needs the perception that will not be the interpreting that becomes a new and pious need for justification in some exposition of life as a whole. Faith is not a part of us that is capable of development. It is not an additional or higher sense achievement (e.g., the organ by which we perceive the intelligible world). It is the bringing of the whole, divinely constituted person into harmony with the salvation of God. In faith we know God as God and ourselves as sinners who exist only by God's action. The perception of faith always expresses itself also, then, as a prayer for the renewing of the unity of all the senses. This is how Paul Gerhardt understood Romans 12:2 when he asked God to cleanse his mind from sin in order that with a pure spirit he might render to God the honor and service that he owed.[8]

The new mind and the sense of Scripture are related then (even by the use of the same word *Sinn* in German). Theologically they belong irrevocably together, for the one cannot be present without the other even though the one is also not to be explained in terms of the other. When the new mind receives God's Word in Scripture it does not congenially produce individual texts as representations of a supratemporal content of meaning. Instead, it sees itself referred to the specific

8. From the second verse of his "Zeuch ein zu deinen Töten" (1653).

message and objective statements of a text. At the same time the promise of God in the biblical words shows itself only to the new mind, the seeing nerve that is integrated into the network of intellectual skin. The new mind is the confidence of hope. Nevertheless, it would be without foundation if a relationship of meaning were derived from a survey of the biblical texts that is independently extrapolated over and above the contexts of the texts and then used in exposition of the individual texts. In that case it would seem as if the biblical sayings were opening up unlimited vistas beyond themselves. But they would then contain only views that would need further development instead of sharpening the new sense.

In this connection we can explain only briefly how it came about in the modern period that the above line of theological understanding was abandoned. I will limit myself to two hints. First, we should note that the request for renewal of the mind has given ground to the question of the origin of understanding in the subject. The subject has thus been forced to satisfy its constitutional need for orientation by an intellectual comprehension of reality. *Sinn* has thus come to denote "meaning for" the understanding subject. Second, textual hermeneutics has taken on a key role for this understanding of meaning. Out of the practice of interpretation there has developed the impression of boundless and linguistically self-enclosed contexts of meaning in which we are always already moving. This impression has been fostered by an understanding of Scripture that views the Bible as a totality that can be opened up by relating individual texts to one another. This conception gave rise to the theology of salvation history, which expounds world history as the execution of the divine plan to save as we find this revealed in the Bible "from beginning to end." Now the meaning is already there over and above exposition of the text. All that we can ever understand is already contained in it.

This prior ranking of a totality of meaning can be seen in the theological contribution to the development of the concept of history.[9] Here the question of meaning has one of its deepest roots as the question of meaning of history relative to its course "from beginning to end."

By its practice of biblical exposition theology came up against textual contexts, related these contexts to world experiences, and then tried

---

9. For details cf. chap. 2 of my *Einführung in die Eschatologie.*

to use them as a key to the understanding of what would come next. When at the beginning of the fifth century the political and intellectual order of the world of antiquity threatened to collapse under the onslaught of barbarians from the North, and doubts arose as to the ability of the cosmos to sustain itself, Augustine set over against a self-resting cosmos his vision of the city of God. He posited fellowship with God as the goal of human history and could thus view world events as the initial movement *(precursus)* in advance to the divine, fixed, and imperishable goal. Along these lines Augustine was not just offering theological aid to his contemporaries in their anxiety about the world but casting doubt on the rightness of their confidence that the world could continue on its own. But it was, of course, less with his criticism than with his view of history that he was the precursor of comprehensive interpretations. For a long time, however, such interpretations were only incidental. They certainly stirred the imagination powerfully and provided perspectives that functioned as a refuge in times of crisis, but there was still no such thing as a total view of history as a connected process of events. If in the programs of salvation history the focus is on world events "from beginning to end," this is because they can be seen as God's work. History is the extension of creation in time (Augustine). God, the Lord of the world, never lets go of what takes place in it. Especially after the coming of Jesus Christ into the world he does not abandon it to some other destiny. This would be the answer to the question of what follows the history of Jesus Christ, and this question was the determinative occasion for asking what the present and future might still mean on the basis of the salvation definitively revealed in Christ. The question of history is oriented to this meaning, which is still the meaning or sense of Scripture. It kindles hope of God's future action in world events and calls for this expectation, which no total view of history can replace.

Nevertheless, the more time passes the more history is not seen as a unit merely because God seeks to work in and by it but because it is the fulfilling of a universal divine will to save. It was inferred from history that the biblical revelation has more value than the stretch of history that has already been left behind. By it more has been experienced than took place hitherto. It seemed logical, then, to think of many areas of meaning separately — for example, the relation of church and state or the expansion of Christianity — and to see in them the key to the evaluating of individual processes and their integration into the course of events as a whole. For what is said in the Bible stands above all history and thus sheds light on the facts of history and lets us see them in a context that no natural linking of events can provide. From this angle the theological study of history sought gradually to understand revelation in a way that would present it as the context of meaning for history as a whole. All events are here related to the purpose that God is pursuing for us to our salvation and to that of the whole cosmos. In relation to this the Bible is interpreted "from beginning to end" as the record of the divine plan for history whose actualizing may be proved as we survey what has thus far taken place and decode events in time.

Speculative approaches of this kind may be found in the many attempts to integrate history, for example, after the model of the seven days of creation, or as the development of the divine Trinity in the ages of the Father, Son, and Holy Spirit, or as a series of divine covenants with the world, with humanity, with God's old people, and with his new people. Such attempts do not merely break history up into periods but permit us to follow it in its course and above all to predict what is still to come, always according to the standard of the biblical sense — so strongly is this related to temporal relations as well. Only from the early eighteenth century did such approaches become increasingly consolidated into the idea of salvation history for the universe. This idea marks an essential step beyond older efforts to view the nexus of world events "from beginning to end" and to find in it the unity of the destiny of humanity and the cosmos. It was no longer content to look at the divine plan in terms of the Bible and with its help to understand all the terrible things that we experience as necessary to salvation and therefore as meaningful.

The springboard was the break in the relation to the world as a perceptible order. The conviction that we can read off the majesty and wisdom of the Creator directly from the "book of nature" as well as the written record of the divine revelation of salvation gave ground increasingly to terror at what Pascal called the silence of infinite spaces. In the course of research that which nature tells us of structures and laws and relations parted company more and more with what we can understand of our own relationships, and in our becoming and perishing we do not see ourselves to be integrated only as anonymous members of independent processes. Since we understand and create order, we have a part in mind and meaning. Meaning is not nonhuman. Only meaninglessness can be that. We thus have a big part in history, and even if we are more driven by it than we can steer its processes, we may at least see ourselves as in relation to those processes and we may appropriate them by way of interpretation. The question of meaning arises in history and not in nature, which is silent on the question. Only in history can we inquire into the agreement of biblical prophecy with actual events. Only here can we see our lives connected to the *universum* whose destiny we share. Conversely, however, history, now viewed as an unbroken web of events and not as a mere sequence of events, is the theater for the fulfillment of the biblical prophecies. History and not nature is the text that we have to decipher to the greater glory of God and to the determining of our own place in the world.

If I am right, then all these things put together form the turning point in the question of the goal of history. It is not by chance that the question of their meaning arose expressly in consequence of this turn. The question presupposes that such meaning is no longer read in, for example, by setting a theologically imposed goal for history, but that it can be disclosed from it by way of understanding. History carries its meaning in itself, and if it is to be a spiritual meaning, history must tell us this itself. It was theology that prepared the way for this transition from textual hermeneutics to world hermeneutics. The transition was not primarily due to a philosophical adoption and translation of older theological views. The meaning of history implies that history itself says what it means, that it contains a message that is certainly in harmony with the total meaning of the Bible but that permits us to expound this meaning only in detail, specifically also in biblical exposition. Then the Bible is understood afresh in the light of history. Its meaning is no longer the pronouncement of each individual history in relation to God's working but the medium of God's revelation. If God speaks to us in the medium of history, that medium has to be a self-contained whole in order to represent God. Only on this premise does it make sense to inquire into the meaning of history, for otherwise it is enough to accept in faith the temporality of existence and its hidden relation to the whole of God's work and the promise of his faithfulness, that is, to place all time under God's verdict.

Theological world hermeneutics, which was soon accompanied by a philosophical one that gradually dissolved it, promoted and developed the question of meaning. Meaning as an intellectual content that is accessible to all human understanding and that is a part of our human self-exposition in the world that is accessible to us seems to be found (if very generally) in history. Meaning here, as in most cases, implies that the world when seen in the round is an orderly one, that contrary experiences can be harmonized with its order, and that conflicting goals of action can be oriented thereto. But it was, of course, no more than two hundred years before the question of the meaning of history became simply the question of meaning in view of the increasing number of open questions and the difficulty of finding completely meaningful presuppositions for the question itself. Already at the zenith of the historical sense, whose role in the rise of the question of meaning we considered elsewhere, the impression grew stronger that there was being repeated in relation to history that which three centuries before had robbed nature of its place regarding the knowledge of God. It seemed to be more and more doubtful whether there is any meaning in history, or the meaning of history is found to depend on the order and goals that we ourselves, appealing to some authority, ascribe to history in order to recognize ourselves again in it.[10]

The question of history's meaning has three features that thus far have suffered no loss from history's dubious significance. First, this question takes into account the beginning and end of history. In particular the end is the goal that gives force to the question. If at every point and in its hidden totality history has its beginning and end in God, the question remains: Which of the things we do or do not do can stand before God? Theologically speaking, the beginning and end are the origin and goal of our temporal experience and action within what happens to us and is done by us. History begins and ends. In the words of Ecclesiastes, we have a sense of this in our hearts. This is not a mysterious native knowledge that we express in our constant inquiring into the why and wherefore. It has reached us as the message of God's creation and new creation. Distinct from this, however, is history's beginning and end as the beginning and end of a continuous process of events and a universal nexus of meaning out of which we cannot fall

10. Cf. p. 69 and n. 21; H. Heimsoeth, *Geschichtsphilosophie* (Berlin, 1948), 76, 87; A. J. Toynbee, "Sinn oder Sinnlosigkeit?" in *Selbstbefreiung durch das Wissen: Der Sinn der Geschichte,* ed. L. Reinisch, 5th ed. (Munich, 1974), 83-99.

as long as we understand ourselves to be moving in it. In that case the meaning of history is the way in which each movement is viewed once beginning and end are grasped. That was how Franz Overbeck, Nietzsche's friend, described the religious view of meaning, and he added that it is theologians who have made the question of meaning a current one and that they are still at work on it.[11]

To avert any poisoning of historical meaning Overbeck recommended that we should ask about the meaning of history in such a way that history can give evidence of its beginning and end to our organs of knowledge.[12] That implies, however, that we must think of history as a positing of meaning according to the measure of human possibilities. Only these boundaries are then set for all projects and perspectives, even for social and political constructions of universal history. Overbeck thus thought that he could restrict excessive growth in this direction by historical criticism. Even if we cannot follow him in this regard, we must at least do him the justice of listening to him when he says of the question of the meaning of history that this question confuses the senses and takes our breath away if it is raised recklessly. It allows us to live if at times we think of understanding it within its limits, letting it encounter us only within the limits that are set for our sakes.[13] The only question is: Where are these limits? They are to be found, I believe, where experience, suffering, and action give evidence that they are meaningfully determined (not foreordained, which would make them insightful on another level). We are limited, but not hemmed in, as regards what is meaningfully accessible to us in time and face-to-face with which we can and should ask whether, as far as we are concerned, it is done or must be undertaken by us at the right time. The limits do not restrict us to what is all too human or to the perspective of an individual experience of history that can be broadened and deepened by knowledge of the historically mediated experience of others. The boundary runs between what is objectively and subjectively meaningful, but we cannot answer for the latter in such a way as to be able to set up the context that seems to be suitable and strong enough for the

11. F. Overbeck, "Christentum und Kultur," from the *Nachlass,* ed. C. A. Bernoulli (Darmstadt, 1963), 5.

12. Ibid., 6.

13. Ibid., 4f.

achieving of the goal of life (as distinct from limited goals). We are always engaged in creating such contexts, whether by way of interpreting, understanding, or ordering. Heeding the sense of Scripture is thus a salutary interruption and must not be evaded by means of some sense that is foreordained for the sense of Scripture.

The limits of the question of the meaning of history that are set on our account also prevent us from absorbing the meaning of life in this question. Far-reaching historical goals or even the idea of an end of history that depends decisively on human action may indeed lead our perceiving and pondering beyond a narrow seeking of security or restriction to the private sphere. But the question of the meaning of life accompanies that of the meaning of history like a shadow. History leaves room for the question of the wherefore of life by letting us imagine a whither of action, that is, meaning in relation and movement to a goal. But if the goal is not reached, if the temporal end (finally death) and the goal do not coincide, then the question of the meaning of life is the more pressing the more it has set a goal for itself or the more severely the supraindividual goals to which life has committed itself transcend this life.

We must remember at this point that the question of the meaning of life in theology, and especially in Christian instruction, replaced an earlier question that viewed the why and wherefore of human life differently. What theology sought was the goal of life that would enable us to know life's origin and end. When Calvin asked what is our chief end, he replied that it is to know God.[14] The meaning, or more soberly the significance, of life is to be, to exist in creaturely fashion, mindful that as special creatures we are asked what is life's goal, and the goal is to know God and to serve him and praise him. True life consists of praise. We have no other goal than to be after our kind, namely, to be responsible creatures before God. That is Heiko Miskotte's exposition of the Reformation catechetical question,[15] and it points us to what the meaning of history might be, "meaning" in a very elementary sense as

14. Calvin's Geneva Catechism (1542) in *Tracts and Treatises,* vol. II (Grand Rapids, 1958), 33: "What is the chief end of human life? To know God."

15. K. H. Miskotte, "Der (Un-) Sinn des Lebens" (1951), in *Der Gott Israels und die Theologie: Ausgewählte Aufsätze,* trans. and ed. H. Stoevesandt and H. J. Weber (Neukirchener, 1975), 145.

the meaning of what is declared prior to any question. This meaning is the basis of the question.[16] History is the extension of creation in time. It offers space and time for the creature's response to the Creator's work.

Implied herewith is not a blind affirmation of life. Yes to the life that is given is as little self-evident as is the joy of Ecclesiastes that comes unhoped for with all the questions that arise regarding the right time and God's work from beginning to end. Those who praise God cease to be self-enclosed. They no longer confront reality pondering and doubting. They can only give thanks, not because they are forced to do so and can do no other, but because spontaneously, and often after many bottlenecks, they assent to what God does and freely find themselves unable to say anything more about it or alongside it.

Aspiring to meaning, then, is part of life itself. It leads to the knowledge of God, to the acceptance not of life as it is but of God's verdict on life as it is lived. This verdict expresses the meaning of life, the incalculable and incomparable significance that it has. Meaning is imparted and measured out to it. It is not the product of a process of life, an attempt to express and communicate it. Even less can meaning be the product of an intellectual mastering of life, of reflection on its given quality that follows existence and reconstructs it as a context of meaning.

The question of the meaning of history has, of course, other roots. It wanted to take all the events that concern us and with which we each have to do and establish them as the context in which the fulfillment of human existence is possible if not actually made the goal. If we relate that to God it means that if God made the cosmos in order to demonstrate his wisdom and omnipotence by its meaningful order, and if nature largely failed to offer this demonstration with and without human cooperation, history is now on the scene as the opportunity to reconcile the disharmony of the world and the incompatibilities of human life in society to the goodness of God. The idea of the meaning of history that we find in the thought of salvation history and in religious philosophy (culminating in Hegel's outlining of world history as the history of spirit) understands history as a process of reconciliation. In

16. How this relates to the transcendental postulate mentioned earlier (p. 74 and n. 5), namely, that every question of meaning presupposes the existence of meaning, is still a problem for the relation between philosophy and theology.

so doing it repeats what was earlier a feature of the religious sense, that is, seeing everything from the standpoint of goodness, so that nothing can be either lost or forgotten. Only that which has lost or abandoned the relation to the total context can be meaningless, only that which evades the integration that is proper to all true historical becoming.

The meaning of history that bids fair to absorb even the meaning of the biblical text is also transcendent vis-à-vis the course of time. It is the radical whither of history, that to which everything ultimately leads. Friedrich Meinecke spoke rather differently of the historical feeling for the transcendent meaning of history. That meaning is the far side of history because we cannot know it within history, but it gives us confidence that all our positings of historical meaning, no matter how fragmentary, cannot remain provisional. If the meaning of history nevertheless carries with it a breath of utopia it is absolutely beyond our reach. It precedes all that has happened, all that can be attained or has not. It confronts brute facts, sets them in motion by the forces it releases, and thus frees them from threatened meaninglessness. Seen in this way, talk about the meaning of history comes within the domain of theology. The meaning of history moves through history like the pillar of cloud and of fire with which God went before his people at the Exodus (Exod. 13:21). Only there is God to be sought, not in the objective meaning of phenomena, nor in historical and social relations, nor in the meaning of life that summons us to have confidence in the life that is given. Instead, the question of meaning draws us into a mood of constant upheaval. As Hans-Joachim Kraus writes, the certainty of mission sets aside the question of meaning, for the question of meaning is a pagan question.[17]

A pagan question? Did we not hear from Nietzsche that it is a typically Christian question? Now it is ascribed to paganism old and new, now to the Christian religion, now to Christianity insofar as it is perverted into a religion and has thus become unfaithful to its task. But as we also learn from Nietzsche, if the question of meaning has become a dubious one, the theme of meaning has not been left behind, for the question can clothe itself in a garment that presents meaning as a

17. H.-J. Kraus, *Reich Gottes — Reich der Freiheit: Grundriss Systematischer Theologie* (Neukirchener, 1975), 305. Kraus owes this statement to his friend Rabbi R. R. Geis.

horizon. Thus there can be direct talk of the opening up of meaning by history and by life that will take place in the coming of Jesus Christ but that already sheds light on all the history that strives toward this goal.[18]

To all appearances the question of meaning has been ousted from theology, but the theme of meaning has been taken up afresh on a different level, namely, that of a shaping of the world that establishes meaning, that is meant to actualize *the* meaning that is opened up for all history and all life. Here the distinction between the objective meaning in all actions and the positing of meaning is abolished in a notion of historical and social action. In this way it is thought that one can counter a nihilistic experience that denies our finding ourselves in an ordered world and our understanding ourselves in it. All that has been handed down is now brought before a forum of criticism that permits us to view the shaping of life only as an action that confers meaning. And past forms of life, including decisions, are measured by what may today be regarded as meaningful.

By this procedure, however, the question of meaning increasingly gains ground and the experiences of meaninglessness are methodically increased. Human suffering is also increased insofar as it derives from pain at a reality that we can no longer experience as without significance. We saw indeed in the passage from Ecclesiastes adduced at the outset that the objective meaning of actions can be debatable and even deeply questionable. But we cannot escape this questionability by trying to construct a context with the help of which we can survey and order all things and in that way justify them. Face-to-face with the crisis of meaning that we feel today, the distinction between objective meaning and the giving of meaning shows itself to be not a merely theoretical distinction that involves problems of orientation. I might say without beating around the bush that the distinction is no less than a matter of faith. This means that none of us arrives at the distinction on our own. Nevertheless, the distinction can and must strike us when we view the alternatives of action as possibilities of life, when we also know of the

---

18. Ibid., 417: "In the parousia of the exalted Christ the kingdom of freedom is consummated. The crisis and meaning of all history and all life will find resolution in this event. . . . The consummation of the kingdom of freedom fulfills the apocalyptic of all servitude and bondage. The disclosure of the meaning of history and life will come with full clarity. But only one event will be determinative: The glorifying of Christ."

context of life to which all such possibilities belong but accept the fact that we cannot grasp the context from the beginning to the end. Thus not only readiness for this is lacking, but lacking above all are the premises on which we can represent this distinction in thought.

If the certainty of being sent to represent God in the world and to take part in the fulfilling of his purposes contradicts the question of meaning, then history as the sphere of the fulfillment of the tasks that are set replaces the given sphere of life thus far marked out. Relying thus on history as it is lit up by the future, we acquire ground under our feet. The existential question of meaning, doubt regarding the basis of our own existence, fear of falling into the abyss, are all set aside by the motif of the way of history. The ground beneath us is no longer shaking because we have been assigned a path on which we can leave behind everything that is destructive and transient and outmoded. A context in which to hide is no longer needed when we are certain of a future that orients all that has happened to itself and gives it value and form. But this future is only a goal and hence our pilgrim task. To reach the goal a new meaning has to be given to life for which the certainty of being sent empowers us. What has happened here? The question of meaning is set aside in order to raise it afresh as the demand to actualize the meaning of history in a world without meaning.

VIII. SENSORY IMAGES

T HERE IS a resistance to the question of meaning that is the last remnant of a long-standing theological opposition to the senses and to an imprisoning of God in the sensory world. It views itself as a fight for freedom from any objectifying of God in the world, and it fears that meaning might eliminate God's transcendence even if in a sublime but for that very reason especially dangerous way. It thus demands that meaning not be identified in the world but that every form of its objectifying remain beyond this world. To keep meaning free for God and God free for final meaning it appeals to God's commandment: "You shall not make for yourself an idol, whether in the form of anything that is in heaven above, or that is on the earth beneath, or that is in the water under the earth. You shall not bow down to them or worship them; for I the Lord your God am a jealous God" (Exod. 20:4f.).

Indeed! The forbidding of representing forces over or under the world (or from the world beyond), or even of wanting to view God in an image of his power, has to do essentially with the question of meaning, though not, of course, in the way that the religion of a utopian sense might suggest when it likes to rely on the Old Testament prohibition of images.[1] The prohibition is not saying that God understands

---

1. Cf. J. Moltmann, "Theologische Kritik der politischen Religion," in J. B. Metz, J. Moltmann, and W. Oetmüller, *Kirche im Prozess der Aufklärung: Aspekte einer neuen*

himself as Spirit far above the world and time and therefore does not will that he be materialized, the general exposition today being that he is the absolute future that is above every historical manifestation and that thus always precedes our world. But this referring to pure futurity (unintentionally) relates to the religious sense that Schleiermacher extolled so highly. As Schleiermacher put it, that which he wanted to know and possess was infinite, and he could fully define himself only in an infinite series of acts. He did not want ever to deviate from the Spirit that propels us forward, and the demand that can never be satisfied by what is past moves ever onward to what is new. It is our glory to know that the goal is infinite but never to stop quietly on the journey.[2] This attitude subjects all that is to meaning from which it must constantly receive its right to exist. The world as it is has no guarantee of meaning that implies its disclosure.

The story of the worshiping of the golden calf (Exod. 32:1ff.) that illustrates the prohibition of images — the image of a bull being a symbol of the divine power of fertility — shows, however, that a sensory representation of God does not threaten his deity, for even an image cannot consign God to visibility. The real apostasy of Israel was the worshiping of another god that was fashioned on the assumption that Israel could invoke him and be sure of his protection. What is contested is not the spiritual nature of God in contrast to all natural powers and forms of life. What is questioned is whether God can be experienced only unexpectedly, or is he represented by a meaning with whose help we can count on him. God, the commandment tells us, wants to see his hiddenness and freedom as the Creator of all things and the Lord of time protected. He forbids symbols because in an image he acquires a presence that can guarantee his being present. Where he is put in an image, not made corporeal but in efficacious reference to him, there can be assurance that he will be present again and again at this place. His presence there becomes a known reality. His essence, of course, will always evade the image, but it will be so tied to it that in the image there is thought to be encounter with God himself. It is in this regard, and

---

"politischen Theologie" (Munich and Mainz, 1970), 38n.57, appealing to E. Fromm, *The Revolution of Hope* (New York, 1968).

2. F. Schleiermacher, *Soliloquies* (ET Chicago, 1926), 96f.

only to this extent, that an image of God promises control over him. To put this in terms of our present subject, we can find God in a meaning that dictates his revelation.

God, however, has nothing in common with such images because he is present and can be known only in a very different way. For us who belong to him he creates space in which we can experience his work in relation to us and to the world. He gives his wandering people signs that they can hold before them in recollection and expectation. These signs are signs of revelation, pledges and promises of fulfillment that take form, but not symbols in which God and the world are interrelated, nor intermediate figures that are neither totally natural nor totally divine. No sensory images can replace God in the freedom of his action, no symbolical entities can be substitutes for his gift of life. Hence none of us may make such images, whether one of the godlike figures that Isaiah unmasks as manufactured things in chapters 40ff., figures in which the religious artist invests all his or her knowledge of divine power but which can still be no more than projections of the human will for power (Isa. 40:18-20) — a criticism of religion that is without parallel even today — or one of the less palpable modern totalities of meaning like history, society, or speech: hermeneutical universals, epitomes of reality out of which we may not fall if we are not to fall victim to nothingness.

The frontier between God and us that the prohibition of images draws is pronounced as a commandment to stay within the living space that God has assigned and as a prohibition against leaving this space, but not as a reflection on the relation between God, humanity, and the world, and on symbolical mediation between them. We are to learn here how to be freed from entanglement in the question of meaning with all its fascination and picture puzzles and yet not at the same time overbearingly to ignore the question. Renouncing the question cannot be based originally on a supposed higher expectation, otherwise it would destroy itself. We can only try to expound this renunciation as a commandment and in this way evaluate it. Three examples will perhaps clarify this as regards our present theme.

The people of God were and are forbidden to turn to death in order to experience the boundaries of existence in such a way as to be able to cross them. Encounters with death never became for Israel the experiencing of a power that manifested God. Contrary to the religions of the surrounding peoples, for Israel the cosmos was not divided into a sphere of life and a sphere of death, with a passage between them that made the way to death one that possibly led closer to God. Israel saw no link between the living and the dead, and any who still sought it found at any rate no disclosure of mysteries in greater immediacy to God (cf. 1 Sam. 28:7ff.; Isa. 8:19). The deceased were excluded from the common praising of God (Ps. 88:10f.; Isa. 38:18f.). They did not go into another world. They were not hurled out of this world in order to be received into the other. Thus the power of death confronted the question of life with God, since death separated not merely from the living but from the fellowship of their service of God. The answer that Israel first heard to this question was a repelling one with no promise of meaning. What death does is not done in its own power. It displays no divinity that might construct a new relationship. The separation of death carries no message. It is not eloquent. We can thus aim at no cultic arrangement with it. God alone speaks to us in both life and death. Hence death in Israel is experienced as God's doing that which we cannot understand merely in terms of a physical end. Death as God's grip can reach us in the midst of life as exclusion from the fellowship of God, not as sudden death.

In the light of the death and life of Jesus Christ, the New Testament speaks more extensively of death in the midst of life as the work of God upon us. In the language of baptism death denotes the existence that is disrupted by God and definitively ended as separation from him; from it the baptized enter into new life. This life has death before it in a new way as compared to those who have not yet experienced death in their lifetime (cf. Rom. 6:2ff.; Col. 2:12ff.). Death as the saving judgment of God protects against the second death that is eternal as an irrevocable falling into nothingness (Rev. 2:11; 20:6; 21:8). This distinction tells us that dying neither annihilates us nor sets us in eternity. Both abiding and perishing are under the verdict of God that reaches us in calling to faith. If in our lifetime we are smitten by the decision of God, eternal death can no longer threaten us, for we have already pressed through (not passed!) from death to life (John 5:24). Time and death are not experienced in the same way as in a being for death that includes the finitude of human existence.[3] The "natural" sequence of life and death is reversed because the living God is encountered in time in such a way

---

3. M. Heidegger, *Being and Time* (ET New York, 1968), 279ff.

that death can no longer be the frontier beyond which the hiddenness of God is lifted.[4]

As I have already indicated, at times the Old Testament describes the experience of death as exclusion from the fellowship of those who worship God. Those who no longer belong to the cultic community are dead, and salvation from death means having the possibility of joining in the worship of God again.[5] But does this mean that experienced fellowship is a social network, that sponsorship by a religious group is a medium of encounter with God? The Old Testament does not draw this conclusion. God's action constitutes the fellowship of faith, but that does not mean at all that the action amounts only to the constituting of the fellowship. Social fellowship persists only as long as each individual in it is exposed to God's action and is ready to be determined by the law of God that is also the basis of the common life. This ranking is binding and may not be reversed. Social action may well be able to set up a relationship with God, but it may also evade God in so doing, as the history of Israel and church history show again and again.

An illustration proving this point may be found in the central celebration of the Christian community, the Eucharist. The living Christ is present "in, with, and under" the elements of bread and wine. Reception of the elements links the community to the destiny and promise of its Lord, integrating it into his death and life in such a way that the Eucharist itself proclaims the death of Jesus until he comes (1 Cor. 11:26). Essential here is the separating of the body of Jesus into the broken bread and the shed blood. What is distributed at the Eucharist is not an intact body, the integrity of a "whole" person, but corporeality that has been perceptibly shattered and that God has created into a new unity that embraces us and gives us fellowship with one another. We basically misunderstand this character of the Eucharist, however, if we celebrate it merely as the establishing of fellowship, as an act of social integration. This view has been thoughtlessly propagated in recent years. Predominant in it is a social need that requires a ritual of establishing meaning. Along these lines the

4. Cf. my "Leben in der Einheit von Tod und Leben," *Evangelische Theologie* 41 (1981), 46ff.

5. C. Barth, *Die Errettung vom Tode in der individuellen Klage- und Dankliedern des Alten Testaments* (Zollikon, 1947), 26, 48ff., 152, 164; G. von Rad, *Old Testament Theology*, vol. I (ET New York, 1962), 387f.

elements symbolize the whole life that is mediated by common sharing in the means of life. Some in the early church misconceived of the elements as a means of immortal salvation, and this misconception repeats itself in the garb of a social interpretation of eternal life as fellowship that is unrestrictedly granted and comprehensively experienced. In this way a "practical" answer is also given to the question of meaning that nevertheless leads precisely away from that which is meant to be promised and imparted to the Christian community in the Eucharist — and not least the opening up of fellowship for all those for whom the death of Jesus took place. The Eucharist is turned into its opposite if it is made a celebration of a fellowship that exists already and of the symbolical representation of this fellowship. Its purpose is not achieved by an establishing of social meaning even though this may be described in terms of religious sociology. The express meaning and purpose of the Eucharist is not restricted to an experiencing of fellowship by those who partake of it. It has point and meaning as a proclamation of the death of Jesus, the reconciliation with God that brings peace to torn humanity, but a peace preceded by the fact that the natural unity of life is broken and we must await the new creation of God.

The example of Job shows finally that a context of meaning that permeates the cosmos, or, in modern terms, a totality of meaning,[6] cannot reveal God. People today like to portray Job as one of the founding fathers of the question of meaning because he did not accept his sufferings but instead protested against them and called God to account for them. His resistance to a fate that made no sense was confirmed by God, and in this way God showed a very different face from that of a distant majesty to which our human suffering is indifferent or that will deign no response to it. Job, then, thrust through to God by way of his suffering. God finally vindicated him and lifted from him the fate that he bore so innocently. Indeed, he logically had to do so.[7] All that happened was simply a testing arranged by the devil to see whether Job had the ability to achieve mastery over that which he could not understand.

6. Cf. R. Spaemann, "Über den Sinn des Leidens (1973)," in *Einsprüche: Christliche Reden* (Einsiedeln, 1977), 123f.: "The question of the meaning of suffering is a specifically biblical question. It presupposes faith in the unrestricted totality of meaning, faith that the universe as a whole stands in a context of meaning."

7. E. Bloch, *Atheism in Christianity: The Religion of the Exodus and the Kingdom*

We cannot discuss in detail here the extent to which this view of the story is defective and the way in which what the story really brings to light is the crisis in the understanding of meaning.[8] I will limit myself to just one aspect: What was Job really asking God? Was his question that of the why and wherefore of his suffering? His friends wanted to lead him to this question (noted above), and they had their final explanations all ready: We must either keep silence before God's greatness because we can never comprehend his will, or we must use good and evil in our lives as an opportunity to cling to the good and in this way bring ourselves into harmony with God. The friends advise Job to reflect on his life as a gift and a task.

This is precisely what Job will not do. He will not commit himself to any contexts of meaning that allow him to explain why he must live the kind of life assigned to him. His friends offer him a way of understanding his fate as one, they think, that comes from the hand of God. To them the action of God seems to be mediated by the constitution of the world and the order of salvation, that is, by the connection between what we do and what becomes of us, by the righteousness of God that responds to guilt with punishment and rewards the fear of God with blessing. God, who in himself is unsearchable, has tied himself to this order in such a way that we can know him in it with no doubts at all. This knowledge of God in terms of the meaning of the world and of individual existence in it is always upheld by the community of those that fear God. The knowledge of God as the friends practice it is actualized in the questions and answers of those who rely on the divine order of meaning as the medium of God, who by way of interpretation comprehend their destiny in the light of it, and who can instruct and correct one another accordingly.

Job rejects this twofold social and cosmic relation. His exodus from

---

(ET New York, 1972), 110: "A man has overtaken, has enlightened his own God. That, despite the apparent submission at the end, is the abiding lesson of the Book of Job"; H. Wiersinga, *Leid: Herausforderungen des Lebens: Auseinandersetzung mit einer Grundfrage* (Munich, 1982), 114: "Job's answer to suffering was more than a protest. It became expectation of a new possibility because he oriented himself to a different God. He appealed to the God who himself will not accept suffering and who wants nothing better than to put things right for us."

8. Cf. H. Gese, "Die Frage nach dem Lebenssinn: Hiob und die Folgen," *Zeitschrift für Theologie und Kirche* 79 (1982), 161, 179.

it stands behind his desire to be extinguished (3:1ff.). He demands judgment and a verdict from God. His challenge to God is that he should speak to him and listen to him and even see him (cf. 19:26f.). He wants justification from God alone, not because God has gone back on what Job expects from him as his Creator and Deliverer, but because he cannot find his life or his salvation in any agreement with the world. He does not ask for a more helpful outcome than his friends can give him; he wants the truth. His question is not whether he can accept his existence when it has proved to be meaningless for all those of understanding. He wants to be justified by God and accepted by him.[9] And the answer of God he receives confirms him, not in his uprightness (that is concealed in time by suffering), but in his unflinching readiness to talk about God's action instead of about a meaning that is advanced when we ourselves fill out by interpretation something that was previously empty or became empty. The encounter with God and the new perception of the world that it brought with it (Job 38–40) show that God's action stands in no relation to what meaning can tell us as an intellectual attempt to understand the world of human life.

9. Ibid., 168f. and 172.

IX. MEANING IN THE
HISTORY OF JESUS CHRIST

T HE BIBLICAL example that I have just adduced seems to run contrary to my earlier thesis that the question of meaning is an accompanying phenomenon of the modern age and even an incidental product of the Christian tradition — the agony of Christian nihilism as Nietzsche saw it emerging. For did not the question of meaning find expression already in the wisdom literature of the Old Testament that also arose in a time of crisis comparable to our own?[1] At that time, too, historical tradition no longer seemed to be sustainable. Individuals no longer saw themselves rooted in the fellowship of the people but thrown back upon very personal questions. Above all, rational mastery of the world proved to be fragile. The order of the world escaped reason when it tried to penetrate it. Like Ecclesiastes, Job accepts the proportions of life face-to-face with all attempts to get to the bottom of the order of things, to see them in their regular courses, and thus to plan life logically and successfully. The bold and confident certainty that we can understand reality and impose purpose on it lay behind them. With a similar critical eye, Socrates at much the same time was refuting the intellectual optimism of Sophism and founding Western philosophy, which soon after, in Aristotle, would lead to limited perception of objective action that we recalled.

1. Cf. O. Kaiser, "Die Sinnkrise bei Kohelet," in *Rechtfertigung — Realismus — Universalismus in biblischer Sicht,* ed. G. Müller (Darmstadt, 1978), 3, 21.

Did not the question of meaning, then, find expression already in those days, and do we not hear it again whenever the foundations of the familiar world begin to shake, for example, when the barbarians attacked the Roman Empire; when Augustine set in antithesis to fear of the collapse of the ancient world the hope of a goal of history, which God had created with a plan and which was striding forward to God's salvation; or at the end of the Middle Ages when face-to-face with profound intellectual and political change Martin Luther found the answer to his question of the gracious God in the justification of the wicked? Indeed, was it not the Christ event itself that revealed the meaning of history at a time when the call for redemption, heard throughout the Mediterranean world, demonstrated that the meaning of life is open to question?

The coming of Jesus into the world as a disclosure of the meaning of history and as a revealing of its significance as world history — this insight means for theology, or, shall we say more cautiously, for a Christian philosophy of history, a thickening of the plot of the question of meaning. We have followed the traces that this question has left behind in intellectual history and in various attempts to expound existence, and in the process we have seen two things. First, what is predominant in the question of meaning is the attempt to comprehend reality in such a way that it alone is understood as meaning for us, as full disclosure. It may be stressed ever so strongly that meaning ultimately transcends us, that we can grasp it only dialectically as the alternation of receiving and generating, of experiencing meaning and establishing it, but meaning always seems to be manufactured and thus bears the mark of what we ourselves produce. Perhaps it is no longer perceived by us unconstrainedly, but it is the form that we ourselves impress upon our encounter with reality. But then, second, the question of meaning arises out of a crisis of the will to establish order in an unfathomable world. It is not originally present. It does not accompany us constitutionally. It is an indication that we are no longer open to the verdict concerning truth and falsehood. Instead we take as reality the relation to reality that we ourselves produce and in which we feel at home.

That we no longer cope with the element of "sense" in the totality of the senses, but increasingly use the senses for this and that and "sense" as an object of these instruments, is something that Nietzsche understood as hardly anyone else. For him the question of meaning arose as a powerful effort, almost too much of an effort, on the part of a culture that is not prepared to deal with the world as it is, and the longer it lasts the more it ceases to be familiar with it. The question develops out of pain and suffering, out of the probing quest for a goal and end that will take from suffering at least some of its sting. Suffering is no longer part of life. It gives sufferers the opportunity of embodying suffering in themselves instead of having to accept it. To the extent that the question of meaning works on suffering, trying to be a match for it, it is of Christian origin, and it differs from all supposedly similar manifestations at an earlier time. The question of meaning as it confronts us today is one of the mortgages left us by Christianity. Its disclosure of the meaning of history and its resultant motivating of attempts at interpretation, namely, its handling of the multiple sense of Scripture, its idea of salvation history as a key to the meaning of all history, its relating of meaning to being that is the basis of the linguistic logic for Christian metaphysics, all these things have given the term *meaning* the double sense that has left the impression of a meaningful world history that is disclosed to us, and that has influenced the consciousness of the West for centuries. History was formerly felt to be a chaos of warring forces and the theater of power that became only for the current victor the stamp that could be impressed upon the conquered world. But now history took on the friendly face of a context of meaning in which all of us can take shelter. Only for a brief time, however, was the fact concealed that this was a face that we ourselves had drawn even when it was maintained that it displayed the features of divine revelation. From the very first the meaning of history as the force that carries humanity was simply an impress of the world of work that is one of the supports of the modern age.

What triggered the crisis of orientation that was intimated for a long time but is now evident was not the secularizing of a Christian view of history into a concept of global progress nor the dissolving of ancient norms and the devaluing or transvaluing of values. These things perhaps contributed, but it is especially the Christian interpretation of history that must carry the full share of the blame. If the coming of Jesus Christ is reduced to that which gives history its meaning, then not only does all history before and outside Christ seem to be meaningless but so, too, does all the world insofar as it does not accept this meaning. This sounds like a faith that sees beyond the chaos of the natural world and perceives an order in it in that our destinies are no longer mere fate but have a disposition for action that is sure of its goal. In fact, however, a chaos is presupposed in order that meaning may be given to it, meaning that expresses our superior vision of the world but also our individual meaning vis-à-vis the world as it is.

Nietzsche, whom preceding theologians had sated with the Christian interpretation of history, became almost uniquely sharp of hearing even to the point of being suprasensory, sensitive to the fatal relationship of goals between the historical desire to understand and the will for power that puts in things a meaning that they do not yield themselves. His mocking of the origins of the Christian faith (*historia in nuce*, as he says succinctly) is much sharper than Goethe's reinterpreting of John 1:1. "The most serious parody I ever heard," he says, "is that in the beginning was nonsense, and nonsense was with God! and God (divine) was nonsense."[2] The beginning was the "place of nonsense: not pure nothing, but falsified, deformed sense, untruth, and falsehood: the birthplace of apparent meaning which covers empty space as with a mantle and conceals it; leading to nothing but not letting it be known as such. Nevertheless, this nonsense 'was' (really and truly 'was'), that is (with God!), it 'has been,' and we are finally done with it and have it behind us. We no longer need to take it seriously, this divine nonsense that surpasses every finite and conceivable measure, for it is no longer."[3]

After this unmasking account there can be no true answer to the question of meaning, for the question can be only apparent. It will produce a significance that covers naked facticity like a protective garment but can never be more than a sham reality. Blown up by the creative ability of individuals and groups into an interpretation of reality, it can reach so far as to give the impression of being a horizon, but in reality it arches like a powerful vault over an artificial world and thus gives us a place in which we can feel hidden as in a mother's womb.

This question of meaning grows out of a hopelessly disturbed relation to our world. Nietzsche tried to trace it as such to its roots, and in so doing looked into an abyss from which he thought he could save

---

2. F. Nietzsche, *Human — All Too Human* (ET Lincoln, Nebr., 1984).

3. F. Ulrich, *Nietzsche und die atheistische Sinngebung des Sinnlosen kritisch betrachtet: Beiträge zum Atheismusproblem der Gegenwart,* ed. E. Coreth and J. B. Lotz (Munich and Freiburg, 1971), 28.

himself only by an absolutely suprahuman leap into pure will. The earlier Nietzsche thought that he could leave the nonsense of Christian history in the West behind him by coming to terms again with the tragic feeling for life that he believed he found in Greek tragedy. But this redemption through the cosmos, the harmony of humanity and the world, did not prove to be humanly possible any more. Nietzsche was not broken on nihilism, in which he found no escape, but on the attempt to leave the terrain of interpretation, on which he found no path. In the process he lost himself in regions that again bear the stamp of modernity. The will for power that Nietzsche proclaimed so emphatically wants to dominate the world in the same way as does an interpretation that covers the world like a net in order to catch it and haul it in for us who can no longer, even together, bear its burden. The need for justification that Nietzsche diagnosed as the driving force behind the question of meaning seeks orientation in a self-created context that is perceptible at all times. Thus the question of meaning becomes the question of idols and its crisis is the twilight of the gods.

Like Goethe, however, Nietzsche missed the point, or ignored it, that in John 1:1 Jesus is the Word. He is this not as the symbol of the power of speech as reality or of the creative power of speech, or as the *logos* as meaning, but as the Word in the beginning, the Word of the primal beginning, God's creative Word, the Word that is communicated and thus defined. This Word was with God. It did not stay with him, however, but moved out from him in order that it might create and sustain the world as this defined Word. The world, then, is not a self-resting cosmos that cannot handle the tragedy of life. It is creation. Creation, however, is not the world that God regards as "good" (Gen. 1:4, 12, 18, 25, 31) in the sense that this verdict stands over against the world as a promise of meaning. In that case a fresh decision would constantly have to be made regarding the goodness of the world. One would have to demonstrate whether it can really be called good. That would then be dependent on a power of judgment that must first establish the harmony between us and the world and that would have to say so if the world no longer deserves to be called good but instead either bad or not yet good. Wherever the concept of perfection has crept into that of creation, the question of meaning has forced itself between the Creator and the creature. This question separates us from the purpose of creation that gives a definite answer to all the questions that have not yet arisen and that is also an imparted meaning which does not need an understanding that integrates the given into a preestablished context of meaning and thus identifies it. Creation cannot be open to this kind of interpretation but is itself original meaning in the double sense of what is given and what may be perceived.

This is why in the Johannine prologue, which refers back to the story of creation, Jesus Christ is the Word that was in the beginning with God, that was God, and that came into the world to reveal God's glory. Now everything depends on creation not being reduced to revelation, on human meaning not being the content of meaning that also hovers over the world, whether to illuminate it or to show what is meaningful in it and what points to its future perfection. To take that course is to validate again the interpretive acrobatics that has led to Christian nihilism and will always do so. The interpreting of the history of Jesus Christ as the disclosure of the meaning of all history is a flight from creation to a history that is not the history of God with us but the context of meaning that we need so as to put the world's filing cabinet and its far-flung references in order. This turning aside from creation as defined meaning is the fall of Christianity. Healing can be sought only where the sickness began. But this place was not, as Nietzsche thought, the nonsense at the beginning of the history of Christian thought, which is irrevocably in the past. It was (and is!) the reduction and restriction of God's gracious creation to what is revealed to me, from which I can then read off sense. If creation is reduced to revelation, then history is made the medium for relations. It becomes the space-time in which the historical consciousness has its recollections and expectations at its disposal. I do not adopt reality and its structure for my action, but must first survey it so as to evaluate what might be possible in relation to what is regarded as meaningful. Doing this is no less than surrendering creation. Only in this way can the question of meaning unfold and do its mischief.

Jesus, however, fully accepted creatureliness. Within its determination he lived and died. He shares God's humanity as the creative Word of God in the body, the Word of which God said: "For as the rain and snow come down from heaven, and do not return there until they have watered the earth, making it bring forth and sprout, giving seed to the sower and bread to the eater, so shall my word be that goes out from my mouth; it shall not return to me empty, but it shall accomplish that which I purpose, and succeed in the thing for which I sent it" (Isa. 55:10f.). That is the meaning of the mission of Jesus. It is all said with his mere existence. He is God's definite Word. He lives and dies thus. His message and work do not point to goals with the attaining of which alone he fulfills his destiny. What he does and what he draws down upon himself simply follow from the fact that he is God's man, as is expressed in agreement with him or in opposition to him. Even his last saying, "It is finished" (John 19:30), is not the assessment of a fulfilled and therefore meaningful life but expresses the acceptance of death, which as God's act upon us is the meaning of our life in union with God.

But is it not playing with words if we exempt the history of Jesus from the question of meaning and then find meaning in it? Perhaps the distinction is hard to see. Perhaps it needs no less than faith to be able to measure it. Meaning defined by God is the given answer that leads to questioning, not the meaning that comes at the end of questions that we raise because we are not open to what is defined for us.

That Jesus of Nazareth is God's given answer may be seen in the way in which he deals with those who feel the burden of the usual questions. Thus we find the man who was born blind and with the cause of whose affliction the disciples wrestle: Did the man himself or his parents sin? Is the affliction an atonement for some wrong that has been committed? Or, as many conjecture, are sick persons, those who suffer meaninglessly, a summons to others to help them to compensate for their physical or psychological defects by other values, and in this way to achieve again the goal of human fellowship on which humanity depends? Jesus has none of such thoughts in mind. He says: "Neither this man nor his parents sinned; he was born blind so that God's works might be revealed in him" (John 9:3). He does not in this way bring to light some mysterious divine meaning for sickness. He says instead that this blind man belongs to God's creation and that his healing makes this definitely clear. If in contrast we ask what is the meaning of useless suffering, this question is measured by a total view of life's goals and purpose. We orient ourselves to a standard of what is a normal and healthy course of life that leaves no room for the question what we can seriously call creaturely life face-to-face with the specific form of life. Those who hold aloof from the question of meaning pose questions. They do not simply accept what they find as it is. They do not merely ask, then, but with their asking they oppose and accuse and protest. Yet with all that we cannot leave the sphere of creation if we do not want to go so far as to accept as objectively meaningful only that whose cause and effect we can see and which we can thus control and direct intellectually.

In the works that Jesus does one may see participation in God's ongoing creation that is ever new. It needs the renewing of the mind to see this as creation. This is the point of Jesus' messianic works: "The blind receive their sight, the lame walk, the lepers are cleansed, the deaf hear, the dead are raised, and the poor have good news brought to them. And blessed is anyone who takes no offense at me" (Matt. 11:5f.). Why the concluding sentence? It is directed against those who have a complete notion of the messianic age, who think they know that it needs a transvaluation of all values to set a hopelessly torn world to rights. On their view the world as it is has to be set aside to make way for God. They cannot see that God has already entered the world in Jesus of Nazareth and that the words and deeds of Jesus are signs of reconciliation to which all further questions about God's coming must be oriented. Because Jesus is not "accepted" (cf. John 1:11), his own people, his fellow creatures, push him out of the world and exclude him from the community of God. Yet the death of Jesus is not a contradiction of his sending. Faced with his end, Jesus prayerfully commits himself to God's will (Matt. 26:39). This shows that here, too, he asks as a creature and in so doing leaves his future to God.

The death of Jesus evokes divided opinions. Does the cross destroy his life's work? For example, Albert Schweitzer suggested that Jesus sought death in order to bring on himself the tribulation of the last days and in this way to usher in God's kingdom and complete his mission. He thus linked the meaning and purpose of his life to a world change. With all the energy of his hopeful will Jesus tried to bring this on by force, throwing himself on the spokes of the wheel of world history. But the wheel crushed him and the cross thus became a symbol of great historical failure.[4] Another view is that God revealed at the cross the higher meaning and purpose of Jesus' life, the divine Yes to the lowly who suffer innocently. Or is the cross perhaps a symbol of the suffering that is only apparently meaningless, so that it gives hope to all other sufferers in virtue of the fact that it did not at all end the significance

4. A. Schweitzer, *The Question of the Historical Jesus* (1906, ET 1909).

of Jesus but on the contrary for the first time disclosed it? Is not Good Friday the transition from the story of the life of Jesus of Nazareth to the history of the revolutionary impact of his message?[5]

These are all profound interpretations, but they are all no more than constructions. They reckon upon a transferred sense, not on God's active and ongoing Word. They allow us to think of a continuing cause of Jesus and even let us conceive of meaning being implanted in the hearts of the timid, who shrink from the terrors of death. Nietzsche called this positing of meaning a stroke of genius on the part of Christianity that even lets God suffer in order to wrest meaning from suffering.[6] One cannot deny that Christian dogmatics and exposition of the Bible and dogmatics have erected a scaffolding of interpretation around the death of Jesus in order to keep Jesus alive in this way. But that is precisely the fatal optical illusion of the Christian understanding of meaning. The life of Jesus is here freighted with questions of meaning. His life is merged into a mission whose meaning we think we can see in a way that makes evaluation of the life possible. His death is then characterized indeed as a crisis of meaning, but we at once pass on from it to a consideration of the continuation of his life in the resurrection and its impact across history. Good Friday and Easter become stations on a connected route that is mysterious but that faith can understand, for every disaster on it is only a provisional crisis and does not rate as an ending in nothing.

Paul, however, spoke of the "word of the cross" (1 Cor. 1:18, RSV) that creates faith in God, "who gives life to the dead and calls into existence the things that do not exist" (Rom. 4:17). The Word of the cross is the Word of creation that was in the beginning, not a bearer of meaning but the created and definite meaning that makes us ask what it implies. As we have stated, this meaning is the basis of our questioning, not as it were the final station (longing) of questions directed at that which we cannot comprehend. It is the abiding subject of human questions, not the solution of problems, nor the fixed point on the far side

5. J. Moltmann, *The Crucified God* (ET New York, 1974), 185f.

6. F. Nietzsche, *Zur Genealogie der Moral*, 2, Aph. 21, in *Werke*, II, 832, in which he speaks of confronting the paradoxical and terrible way in which humanity has found alleviation for its torture, the master stroke of Christianity, God sacrificing himself for our guilt, God himself making payment to himself, God the only one who can resolve for us that which cannot be resolved by us.

of all crises of meaning. The cross of Jesus Christ does not open up the meaning of world history in the absolute. It is not a set of crosshairs that enables us to locate and integrate everything that takes place in the world. It is a sign of God's history with us that has been set up in the world, the word of reconciliation (2 Cor. 5:19). It puts an end once and for all to the kind of question of meaning that loses itself in shoreless space-time, in all the heights and the depths, the past and the future. In place of the primal confidence that experience of meaning is supposed to grant, and that is sought by us in our quest for meaning as a kind of elixir, or so experts in religion and social psychologists assure us, there now comes "hoping against hope" (Rom. 4:18). We are summoned to have confidence in God's ongoing action against all the possibilities that we can foresee and perceive.

To ask after meaning now implies discovering the presence of the cross of Jesus. We have to listen to the questions that are enclosed in the death of Jesus, questions that human thinking in place and time cannot stand up to, questions as to our place before God, the promise of life and destiny of death, the oneness of God's judgment and salvation, the old and the new in God's history with us. Can "history" continue after this death, can it simply go on its way, or does this death pose the question how there can be any history at all if it can no longer be made up of human expectation and recollection? Christian theology shows already in its beginnings in the New Testament from how many different angles it constantly comes up against this question, and not merely once but again and again begins to state it clearly enough. The development of Chistian theology may be misunderstood as a powerful attempt to master Good Friday, as an effort, grandiose perhaps but often contradicted by the actual course of events, to see the factual sequence of history since that time in the light of the Good Friday event, and then to understand all that precedes it as prehistory. It is not the course of history as we perceive it, however, that enables us to accept the "word of the cross." On the contrary, "history" is disclosed here in a way that makes it possible for the first time for our questions to be vital movements. The movement is that of the question imparted in the cross of Christ, of *the* question that is put to the coming God as it opens itself to his working. Hence the cross of Christ cannot be a kind of Archimedean point that we might attain to by a strenuous effort to understand or a change of intellectual position. Nor is the figure of Christ a symbolical one whose features we can transfer to similar situations in life. Even the suffering Christ is not a symbol, not even the symbol of suffering as the key to human existence. The New Testament description of the death of Jesus as "sacrifice" shatters all such interpretations. In this sacrifice human life comes into contact with God's action in such a way that this action in this life is wholly God's Word, God's self-communication.

Thus the suffering and exalted Christ is present in the word of the cross. He is not made present by interpretation. Instead, Jesus Christ speaks in the word of the cross. He does so in a way that makes it possible for us to perceive the meaning appointed for us. The New Testament at times puts this in a universal and apparently very summary way. Participating in the destiny of Jesus, we are dead but believe that we shall also live with him (Rom. 6:8). "If anyone is in Christ, there is a new creation: everything old has passed away; see, everything has become new" (2 Cor. 5:17). These categorical assertions make the decisive point: You are dead, the old has passed away. This is the appointed meaning that we have to perceive, and to perceive not merely generally, as a truth that has been at some time planted in history and that now casts its light on the surrounding terrain of all other stories of human lives. If that were the intention it would lead to the unanswerable question of meaning: why it had to happen at this place and time and in this form when it really ought to have happened much earlier, or perhaps much later so as to enable us to answer by means of it the problems to which post-Christian history has given rise.

Even though the New Testament might seem at times to think and inquire along such lines, on closer inspection the texts speak a totally different language. Thus Colossians 1:24 refers to Paul's own completing of what is lacking in Christ's sufferings. Are we for this reason to view world history as an unending history of suffering? Are we even perhaps to see here an explanation why history has to continue after the death of Jesus? That would be reading off from the cross of Jesus a meaning that we might then attach to this or that affliction in order to make it bearable or at least understandable. But the death and resurrection of Jesus Christ do not change life in this way into suffering, as though our opposition to God and Jesus Christ whom he has sent were the law of all that happens. This contradicting and opposing may well continue and perhaps become even stronger, but they are not the key to an

understanding of history. The suffering typified by the death of Jesus
does not have to be repeatedly experienced. In suffering we have to
discover that life means above all letting what is decisive happen to us.
In this lies perception of the appointed meaning.

The appointed meaning is God's self-communication in his Word,
in the Word which is not information about something that has to be
interpreted to be understood, but in the Word that is wholly self-
communication and the self-communication that is wholly Word.
Communication means that to be understood this Word does not need
any medium to give it its content. The communicated meaning is the
definition in relation to which what is objectively meaningful can be
spoken. There is no referring of the objective meaning to a meaning
behind it that we must first fathom if we are to identify detailed
happenings. We do not discover this meaning or build it up by arranging and structuring. The presence of Jesus Christ contains the relating
of all of us to life and death, to God and the world and one another.
This existing structuring is communicated to us; it is for us to discover
and to recognize it.

We can see how this happens in the Pauline epistles. As paradigms
of the perception of the presence of Christ in the word of the cross,
these are the exact opposite of an interpretation that takes the life and
death of Jesus to be significant elements with whose help we can as it
were restructure our own existence and thus make it understandable.
There is certainly "understanding" in Paul, but only in the sense of
accepting and appropriating what is communicated to us, and not to
us in the mass but to us as individuals, as members of the body of Christ
with all our very different experiences. The experience of fellowship
with Jesus Christ takes place in the opposition of life to death. Participation in the history of Jesus Christ is constituted by this irremovable
antithesis, and it is so, indeed, in such a way that the reality of the death
of Jesus and the hopeful presence of his life may be seen in various
people who then find themselves referred to one another:

> For we do not proclaim ourselves; we proclaim Jesus Christ as Lord
> and ourselves as your slaves for Jesus' sake. For it is the God who said,
> "Let light shine out of darkness," who has shone in our hearts to give
> the light of the knowledge of the glory of God in the face of Jesus
> Christ. But we have this treasure in clay jars, so that it may be made

clear that this extraordinary power belongs to God and does not come from us. We are afflicted in every way, but not crushed; perplexed, but not driven to despair; persecuted, but not forsaken; struck down, but not destroyed; always carrying in the body the death of Jesus, so that the life of Jesus may also be made visible in our bodies. For while we live, we are always being given up to death for Jesus' sake, so that the life of Jesus may be made visible in our mortal flesh. So death is at work in us, but life in you. (2 Cor. 4:5-12)

The final sentence outlines the vicarious experience of the presence of Christ and shows that Paul is not measuring the fellowship of Christ's sufferings by a similarity of fate. In this way he wants not merely to resist any uniformity of experience, as though we could repeat in some way the life and death of Jesus, but positively to state that his suffering has the purpose of making the glory of God visible. He sees himself referred to God's work in the world, and this work is done as people find out that by their suffering, human guilt before God and the reconciliation of the world to God are manifested, so that we can accept the denial of our existence by others as the work of God. We are not explaining suffering, not even as the consequence of sin, or at any rate not in such a way that, achieving comprehension by means of this explanation, we rise above suffering and can accept it as meaningful because it takes place with some higher goal. No, we accept it for what it is, acceptance of God's action upon us, an event that points to God himself. Sufferers who accept their affliction as a manifesting of the defined Word of God direct the attention of others who see them away from themselves and point them to the God who is at work on them.

This implies, however, that meaning is no longer restricted to the significance that attaches to an event, experience, or action because it speaks to us like a text. Meaning is related primarily to perception. It is not that all that happens to us depends on how we perceive it, but that perception orients itself to the specific meaning and is shaped and transformed by it. Perception of specific meaning is a tiring and often painful process. For with it there takes place the transforming of our human power of comprehension into the new mind, into attention to God's Word. The specific meaning of the history of Jesus Christ, the word of the cross, strikes home to our mind, to our power of judgment which embraces all sense perceptions but also all the questions that arise

out of experienced reality. This power of judgment is itself created anew
by the word of the cross in order that the mind may receive this word
and let itself be directed by it. "Let the same mind be in you that was
in Christ Jesus," says Paul in Philippians 2:5, and he is not referring to
a religious sense that seeks to reach above the earthly world to heaven,
to embrace the depths of existence, and to hover above the unfathoma-
bilities of a world that we can no longer comprehend rationally. Nor is
it some spiritual sense that is implanted in certain elect people, nor a
higher sense as a sense for higher things that can attract to itself and
consecrate the mere words of a text or the linguistically constituted
givenness of a process or event. Nor is it a sense mysteriously concealed
behind things and words and needing to be worked out. No, the new
mind perceives what God causes to be communicated to the world. It
is faith's power of judgment that justifies God. To justify God is to give
up self-justifying, to be satisfied with God's hidden action, and thus to
enter into the movement of the question that is addressed to the coming
God.

Paul called the mind that directs us in all our actions and hopes
phronēma, that is, consideration directed to a goal (we are reminded
again of Aristotle's meaning of action), and the power of judgment that
can evaluate one's own conduct and that of others — in short, the mind.
But if what is being expressed here is that the new mind is not the
cognitive act of individuals (which may take into account the insights
of others but is originally rooted in subjectivity), that it is instead the
unity and unifying of perception, then the concept of consensus comes
into play.[7] For each individual, consensus sums up all that encounters,
embraces, and moves that individual.[8] In this consensus we acquire
anew the judgment that enables us to live consciously even as the
distinctions meet us in which our existence moves at the sensory level.
As the language of Christian faith calls this consensus the renewed mind,
the perception that God has created afresh and transformed, it sees the
power of judgment related to this consensus as the integral act of

7. Cf. my article, "Consensus," *Theologische Realenzyklopädie,* ed. G. Krause and
G. Müller, vol. VIII (Berlin and New York, 1981), 182ff. (with bibliography).

8. Corresponding is what Aristotle calls anthropological *sensus communis;* cf. its role
in the psychology of Thomas Aquinas, on which see E. J. Ryan, "The Role of the 'Sensus
Communis' in the Psychology of St. Thomas Aquinas" (diss., Carthage, Ohio, 1951).

concurrence, integration into God's action.[9] But in this way consensus reaches beyond individuals and becomes common agreement, concurrence in the specific sense that enables individuals to recognize the mode of their participation in the history of God with us.

Theologically consensus means the common mind, though not in the same way as in the history of sociophilosophical concepts, which speaks of a *sensus communis* in antiquity in the sense of human consensus, or the agreement of a majority, as a criterion of truth.[10] On that view, which has been adopted again in our own day and been made into a theory of truth as universal fellowship in language, consensus implies a human agreement that leaves no room for further questions. Each real consensus, embedded in the social structure of our world, is the finding of meaning. And meaning is conditioned by the possibility of achieving such agreement, and also expresses what is conceivably the final justification of what we embrace in concert because we pursue it in concert.

The consensus of faith is different. It concurs with what God creates as a unity in distinction from the agreement that rests on community. The consensus of faith expresses the communion with what God has defined as meaning. It accepts God's Word and holds fast to its promise. It is the expression of participation in God's reality in the communication of life with Christ. It is this expression in the multiplicity of the Christ experience, which can be perceived only in faith, not in the "unison" of the religious sense, which as the supreme unifying sense is supposedly common to us all and can thus vouch for the final unity of all our experiences of this world and the next. The consensus of faith lets God in his goodness have the last word. It consists of recognition of God's right to his creation and to the human race.

What is the bearing of this on the question of meaning? Might it be that the consensus of faith is expressing the givenness of the world and life as the meaning of existence, again along the lines of the sociophilosophical concept of the common mind as the world's linguis-

9. Luther prepared the ground for this understanding of consensus in his debate with Augustine regarding the exposition of Rom. 7; cf. R. Hermann, *Luthers These "Gerecht und Sünder zugleich,"* 2nd ed. (Gütersloh, 1960), 139-233.

10. K. Oehler, *Der Consensus als Kriterium der Wahrheit in der antiken Philosophie und der Patristik: Eine Studie zur Geschichte des Begriffs der Allgemeinen Meinung* (1961), reprinted in *Antike Philosophie und byzantinisches Mittelalter* (1969), 234-71.

tic development as it is now present for us? The religious variant would
be an absolute concurrence with the world as it takes place as history,
the consensus that accepts all that happens, so to speak, as God's out-
working. This is in fact the way in which people often expound the
question of meaning that addresses the meaning and purpose of life.
The question concerns reality as a whole, and it finds an answer in a
confidence in existence that relies on life as it is and thus follows up its
wealth of relations, and by experiences that are increasingly comprehensive approximates to life's fulfillment. In contrast the consensus that
comes with the transforming of the mind and its power of judgment
unveils as a false conclusion the apparently devout principle that all that
is comes from God. The renewing of the mind first asks what is God's
will, what is good and acceptable and perfect (Rom. 12:2), realizing the
disability of the world, the hiddenness of God's activity in it, in its mix
of joy and pain, because no perfection is as yet granted to us. It is not
for us to conceive of a God who stands above good and evil and thus
embraces the totality of the world in himself in such a way that we come
up against him everywhere. No, it is for us to ask what is good but
without calling evil meaningless or withstanding it in our own power
because it stands under God's judgment. In consensus, meaning does
not come to expression as the final and basic agreement with the self
as agreement with its world,[11] whether individually or socially. Consensus is anchored in God's specific work, and it trusts in the God who is
not all-determinative reality in such a way that all of us, if we seek
broadly and deeply enough, may find ourselves absorbed in him. Consensus has to do with the reconciling action of God, who will not let
his humans and his world fall from his hand nor let them be separated
from him. To inquire into meaning is to be referred to this consensus
and to be upheld by it.

11. Welte, *Auf der Spur des Ewigen*, 22.

X. GOD OR IDOLS?

TO TEST this orientation to meaning in the history of Jesus Christ we might mention by way of example the attempt to make Jesus the model of a meaningful life. "Hans Küng Answers the Question of Meaning": so read a newspaper heading, though how much of the account must be ascribed to the reporter I cannot say.[1] The report begins with the customary lament at the loss of values and goals in our day and includes a reference to the crisis that has overtaken all authorities, whether state, church, or family.

We then read that liberalization and the ending of taboos were necessary but that they have gone so far that every form of support or orientation is now open to question. The unrest among young people also involves a great crisis of meaning. We cannot set up a new order of meaning by reason alone. Why not lie, steal, or kill? No ethics can be built up on discursive arguments. We certainly have plenty of rules, but in a world that is changing more quickly than ever before there is no basic or lasting orientation. As substitutes we find sects, biorhythms, horoscopes, practices of meditation. The Christian offer of meaning puts to all of us the decision whether there is for us any primal meaning or value, whether we dare to trust. In Küng's view practice shows why this faith is meaningful. Those who refuse to make this decision decide irrationally for other values, career, money, sex, or some other idol that cannot provide any

1. *Basler Zeitung vom Mittwoch*, 2.18.1981, 39.

143

meaning that carries weight. But what is the origin of the basic orientation? Küng referred to Jesus Christ of Nazareth, who as a historical figure
bore witness to his God. This is not an overseer God, a legal God, a God
of males, judges, and kings. This is a Father God with maternal traits, who
loves and who accepts even the weak and unsuccessful. He is not a God of
the powerful who offer the disadvantaged the promise of better things in
the next life. Küng then depicted the implications for living. Sharing,
serving, and renouncing with no hope of return are self-evident. The
witness of the living Christ shows us how we today can be truly human
and can thus give back meaning to our lives.

All these may well be inspiring words, but are they not interpretations
under which Jesus Christ is buried anew? Do we have here the word of the
cross that pronounces the wicked righteous, forbidding them to justify
themselves? Perhaps the offers of a new giving of meaning that crop up
more and more under the sign of a crisis of meaning and with a stamp of
religious goodness do not seek to go that far. But even if they are only
offering help in orientation, it has to be clear to what they are really
pointing. Does not Küng's reply to the question of meaning express the
wishful thinking of an all-embracing security? On closer inspection this
is achieved by what is, in political terms, a human solidarity for which God
vouches as he is communicated in his sustaining significance by Jesus of
Nazareth. And the fact that this God also has maternal traits is not a small
concession to feminist objections against God the Father but follows
logically from the question of meaning itself. God stands for acceptance,
for sheltering love, for carrying across all the abysses of life.

The question of the meaning of life is a symptom of the concern
for security, which can also be achieved by interpretations. Here once
more we come up against the effort to refashion the world as creation.
Many modern sociological theories have tried to make this plausible by
constructing a valid framework, which will be reality for us, out of the
chaotic variety of things that flow down upon us. Reality is then the
totality of meanings that apply to the individual or to humanity as a
whole and toward which we direct our senses, and especially understanding as a general sense, and if the two things, significant reality and
the understanding individual, coincide, then totality has been achieved
and there is the agreement between the self and the world that we
mentioned earlier as a definition of meaning, and that can also describe
the process of giving meaning.

Meaning as this kind of totality: Why can we not be content with that and rely on it? But few answers to the question of meaning can help to remove the crisis of meaning by an orientation that promises to make life bearable, that even point beyond it and in this way enable us to master many things in life that are not bearable. Thus the meaning of existence that we seek has to be a meaning that does not simply accept as an unalterable fact the existence of the other whose life we share. It must also be a meaning that takes into account the fact that the human race exists as a whole, a meaning that shows why it is better that this is so than that it should not be so.[2] The question of meaning is raised here because the fact of humanity cannot be a meaningless one if we are not to cut the ground from under what is done in the race and by it. Why is anything here at all? This ancient philosophical question, the primal question of metaphysics, recurs now in relation to the need that humanity has for meaning. It is raised again by the need for action and the threat to it posed by experiences of meaninglessness. Why is humanity there as it is, namely, driven by the need to act and also unalterably limited by the death of each individual and fear of the ending of the world by human action?

The answer that the philosopher Hans Reiner gives to this kind of question has religious, ethical, and social dimensions. It is as wide-ranging as conceivable, and yet it amounts to no more than repeating the fact of human existence in the form of the giving of meaning. The Christian answer, he says, is that the human race and all creation exist to honor and glorify God, that this goal is God's work in creation, and that meaning is thus given to human existence.[3] Put philosophically, this means, he says, that we are not to seek the meaning of the existence of humanity as a whole merely in the good in humanity but also in the task of actualizing the good that is set for it.[4] Comprehensively, meaning then consists of an explanation of human existence in terms of its reference to this work of actualization and also to others as the horizon of this action. Existence means being there for something (the goal of creation, or, in terms of metaphysics and ethics, the actualizing of the good) and being there for others. If we see the meaning of our existence in our tasks and our being there for others, then we can also experience

2. H. Reiner, *Der Sinn unseres Daseins*, 2nd ed. (Tübingen, 1964), 46.
3. Ibid., 51.
4. Ibid., 61.

victory over the threat to this meaning that death poses.[5] For humanity as a whole and the good as the primal ground of all meaning take up each individual human life into themselves as a meaningful part of reality.

We have to object to Reiner's answer to the question of the meaning of life that it reflects reality itself. That is, the givenness of humanity and the facticity of human action are so transferred into intentions that they can apparently serve to orient individual actions and relations to others. What exists becomes a definition of meaning that supposedly gives direction to what exists. But does it really do so? It would seem to the contrary that such answers to the question of meaning hardly admit of differentiation. They seek to disclose meaning, to give meaning to existence as a whole, and they leave the impression that everything that can be experienced and done in this framework is meaningful, yet they leave nothing as it is, but dissolve everything into a totality of meaning, and above all they load all expressions of life so heavily with the extracting of meaning that only all or nothing can be experienced and actualized.

If we put the question in such a way that it can be silenced only by answers in which the reality we can see reflects itself with all its promises and needs, then we sacrifice many individual factors in the universal question of meaning that have only limited objective meaning. We do so because we cannot fit them in. To see the meaning of our existence in our tasks and our existence for others no doubt sounds like a perfect ethical rule, but quickly this demand that is made upon our existence can turn into a pitiless subjection of individual life to murderous ends in the common interest and in the service of the final goal of society or some other value. And the task of actualizing the good can soon impose an intolerable burden on human action if this is no longer, as in Aristotle, oriented solely to the good but is supposed to produce the good, as though the good were not a qualification of each specific action but the essence of each meaningful action!

The universally posed question of meaning leads to total answers and turns out to be a question of idols. When God is held up as the universal context, or the totality of meaning, or ultimate meaning (all different definitions of the same thing), he is an idol mirroring and reflecting those that produce him. And this idol becomes a Moloch

5. Ibid., 41.

engulfing those that produce him in the goals and values ascribed to him. This may be seen also and precisely in religious answers. To say that the human race, like all creation, exists to honor and glorify God, that this goal is the work of God in creation, and that it thus gives human existence its meaning, is to give an orientation to a meaningful life that expresses a piety which again and again sees in the cosmos indications of the God who has creation praise its Creator in its simple existence, as the psalmist says: "The heavens are telling the glory of God, and the firmament proclaims his handiwork. Day to day pours forth speech, and night to night declares knowledge" (Ps. 19:1f.). But if the world is to have the *meaning* of glorifying God, it can no longer serve its Creator as *creation*, but serves the *goal* that he has set for the world with its creation; and with the laying down of this goal, we have to object theologically that its character as creation is abandoned. Creation must not become a goal for which it was created, for that would mean its degradation to the status of a means to an end. According to the will of God and in the eyes of God it is an end in itself. In God's judgment it is good (Gen. 1:31). Thanks to this goodness it can praise God as long as it is not prevented from still being creation. But this praise of God is on a different plane from the question of the meaning of the world and all answers to it. The praise of God cannot become a question of that kind, for it consists of joy at the union of the work of God with what takes place. This is the place of the joy that Ecclesiastes mentioned earlier, the joy that made him ask after meaning but would not let him investigate meaning as an observable nexus of possibilities and reality. It was in the tension between asking, not so much for *the* meaning as for the will of God, and the promised work of God that there arose for him the joy of having his share in it.

In matters of meaning, then, what is at issue is the world as creation and humanity as creature. Is the world a construct of meaning, so related to human understanding and forms that we think of "meaning" as a medium that enables us to see our part in the coming into being of reality? This kind of concept, which characterizes unforeseeable connections and comprehensive relations, touches on our creaturehood. We know about connections and relations. They are put in our hearts, as Ecclesiastes says (3:11). He could see this in questions about the right time arising out of the appointed time. It can be seen, as we must continue with reference to the cross of Christ, in the specific word, God's action with us as we accept dying as well as living as God's will and orient all human recollections and hopes to it. But the relations and connections that are thus disclosed are not given in such a way that we can make them productive and creative for us and ourselves for them. Meaning is never to be received as though we saw in front of us a task by performing which we arrive at the ground of our existence. It is not as it were an empty page on which we are to draw lines (structures of meaning) that we must then fill in. Instead, meaning is limited to what we find to be defined, including our own perception. As we stay in this field of vision, we honor the Creator by accepting ourselves as creatures, as those who, knowing, do not know, finding traces of the context of things but unable to see the whole "from beginning to end." In contrast, positioning a total meaning for life and the world seeks to awaken confidence by comprehensively integrating things. But in the process "sense" ceases to be perception, attention amounts to no more than interpretation, and interpretation wants to be more than accepting the appointed meaning.

The slender but vitally important boundary between perception and explanation — the distinction is decisive but it is often ignored in the quest for meaning — comes to light when we consider critically how interpretations come into being. In our own trains of thought we have learned to relate interpretation mainly to orientations to a totality of meaning. Answers to this question of meaning in particular seek a final, total meaning of this kind. In Ecclesiastes and Aristotle, however, we note that the perception of meaningfulness differs from being able to offer an interpretation. For real and not just imagined orientation this is a decisive difference. We may, like Ecclesiastes, receive the meaningfulness of an event, experience, or action with the fact itself, so that the question of the "right time" can make the union of God's action and our life its starting point, or a total meaning may be defined in advance, and no matter how pious it may sound, the concrete question no longer arises for us because the relation between God and us and the world seems to be regulated by a nexus of meaning. Here is the reason why we cannot follow the saying of Nietzsche and go back from sense to the senses, why sense or meaning as the specific meaning of God's work, and to that extent the orientation of our perceptions, rules out any self-justification of existence, any grasping and understanding of meaning as totality outside of which we can conceive of nothing else, instead of letting our own mind be renewed.

In paraphrasing Ecclesiastes 3:1-15 I said that the author stopped at a crucial point and asked no more questions. This does not mean that he had become too skeptical to pursue vital questions further. He stopped for a specific reason, that is, when he noted that the search for a context "from beginning to end" by which to assess all reality and thus to justify one's own action might turn into an actual need for self-justification. Because he saw the question of meaning in its absolute and universal sense to be a forbidden one, he could raise different questions and turn to a different kind of knowledge, the perception that led him to joy in the goodness of God. The meaning of God's hidden work replaced the question of meaning.

All this is very different from an archaic capitulation face-to-face with the question of meaning. Nor was it modesty at a time when people could still believe because God was self-evidently present to them as Creator or however nostalgic records might depict him. Ecclesiastes is an eloquent example to the contrary. He knew the pain of an unremitting question as to the order of the world, as to an explicable context of working and suffering, as to the unavoidable evil consequences of the best intentions. He did not forbid himself further questions because he could find no answer for them. Nor did he deceive himself with the argument that we should let final questions stand, and that only thus can we be eloquent and honest. No, he did not set aside such questions in that way. He realized instead that it was only brokenly that he could see the direction of such questions as long as he tortured himself in trying to find a context that he could control. Human inquiry is oriented to "the right time," to the coinciding of our suffering, experiencing, and acting with what God does. It is with this orientation that we must ask constantly what is God's will, what is the good, the acceptable to God, and the perfect, as Paul would later say (Rom. 12:2). This question cannot be replaced by an answer to the question of meaning, plausible though that might seem, for knowledge of meaning would involve for the world the exclusion of all that is meaningless and chaotic from "reality for us."

Those who expect an answer to the question of meaning, then, are bound to be disappointed. The inexhaustible activity of interpreting that creates meaning and understanding that sees and integrates all details on the basis of a total meaning in which all human expressions of life are embedded, or, finally, being itself in its inexhaustible fullness and strength

— these might be the real or unreal things that can all too quickly answer the question of meaning, of absolute sense. Secretly or openly, such an inquiry will at least reproduce the constitution of the world, if not build up this constitution from the very foundation. Perhaps the question of meaning as it is generally put today will not always go to such depths or rise to such heights. But on closer inspection one will see that even apparently more modest and limited answers are commonly rooted in an expectation that focuses on no less than the meaning of the totality of the world, or on that of human history, life, and work. This meaning, it is thought, will have to disclose itself before any detailed experience or activity can be investigated, evaluated, or weighed.

But with the question of meaning we founder (to reverse the concluding words of Goethe's *Tasso*) on the rock that we ought to climb. The question of meaning is immeasurable and arrogant. Along the lines of this question two results are possible and even impressive and fascinating, but they lead us to a positing of meaning instead of to openness to given meaning. To ask for absolute meaning means that we cannot inquire into objective meaning as Ecclesiastes did, and also in his own way Aristotle. Precisely by not putting the question of meaning (though it at least announced itself in Ecclesiastes) they could seek meaning in another way and put questions from which they would have been otherwise debarred. To ask after meaning thus means first of all to perceive the direction in which to ask in such a way that the question does not already anticipate the answer. To be sure, hermeneutics has taught us that the concept of meaning shows that we cannot ask in the void because there must always be some preunderstanding of what can lie within the bounds of the question. The question, it seems, can only go to meet that which has already made itself known and which gives rise to the question. For this reason, does there not lie behind the question of meaning the promise of finding it, even though, of course, we do not yet know where and how?

Now it is true that the quest for meaning has humanity and the world to deal with, and it is not, therefore, without foundation. It stays with things that can be talked about: in the case of Ecclesiastes the unavoidable contrariness of all that takes place and is done, in Aristotle the intentional structure of all actions. On such observations all knowledge that goes beyond mere impressions or sense responses rests. That we can measure such relations and make distinctions is expressed in the anthropological concept of meaning with which we started and to which we have constantly returned. Corresponding to this meaning is the meaningful nature of the world in which we live, which we perceive, in which we move with our questions, and to which our many answers and questions apply. It was in this direction that biblical wisdom had and passed on its experiences, as did also a philosophical collection and arrangement of meaningful references on which Western thought built fruitfully for a long time before it undertook a comprehensive reconstruction and establishment of its own world of meaning. With this turn, however, came the concept and the related question that promise to vouch for the world as it is in its totality, including what may become both of it and of us. But this is no real promise. Crises of meaning have thus arisen that differ basically from previous catastrophes because they no longer shake only the familiar structure of the world. They arise because we are shattered when we can no longer trust our senses face-to-face with what we have created and set up as meaning.

When Nietzsche issued the slogan "Back from sense to the senses" he wanted to entrust himself to the cosmos that is self-resting, that embraces all possibilities, and that is therefore meaningless. But in the process he could only offer another meaning that differs from traditional interpretations because it more radically abandons the world as creation. The question of meaning takes offense at the constitution of the world and of human existence in it. It wants to break the given structure, to take hold of it (religiously), and in this way to disclose a reality that is not just there on its own behalf but serves higher ends. Alternatively, it seeks to cast us back upon facticity in such a way that we rely (nihilistically) only on that which we have posited in it.

This study has been trying to propose a different path, namely, to characterize meaning as perception deriving from the creatureliness that is directed by God himself to his coming. Thus the question of meaning may be stamped by a knowing not-knowing, that is, knowing that the world does not move dumbly around in circles but that we may see in it that which sustains and upholds it, God's creative working. As Ecclesiastes noted, meaning derives from the fact that the creative world has objective meaning in its time. It has meaning as meaningful time in its relation to God's action, the hidden action of God that does not confront the world as its idea or control it as a critical principle. Meaning may be perceived as a trace of God's action in its free working. The question of meaning as a searching quest for the why and wherefore is taken up into the question of the whither of our human path in this world that is so unfathomable.

> You must not go according to your understanding but beyond it. Sink into non-understanding, then I will give you my understanding. Non-understanding is the true understanding. Not to know where you are going is really to know where you are going. . . . Look, this is the way of the cross, you cannot find it. I must lead you as if blind. Therefore not you or anyone or any creature, but I, I myself will give you direction as to the path you must take. Not the work that you choose, not the suffering that you think up, but that which comes upon you contrary to your own choosing, thinking, or desiring, is the way. There follow, there I call you, there be a disciple, there is the time, your master has come.

This is how Martin Luther expounded the saying of God in Psalm 32:8: "I will instruct you and teach you the way you should go. I will counsel you with my eye upon you." And he took the concluding words to mean that our eyes should be upon us as God's eyes are open and upon us. Luther translated "instruct" as "give understanding," and this shows that by "nonunderstanding" he did not have irrationality in view but presumably the power to posit and establish meaning for the world contrary to God's own indication of the path.

Everything is perverted, however, if out of this we derive a meaning that can be lent to life and establish it by interpretation. What is incalculable and unfathomable and a matter of chance would then hold forth as meaning. The intention is not to worship the contingent or purely factual. What is advocated is the attentiveness that refrains, even if often with obvious difficulty, from seeking answers to questions that look for meaning solely in sketches of the world and life that have to be worked up step-by-step. Creation, and all creatures in their own existence, have meaning in the hands of the Creator, their own specific meaning. To perceive our existence in such a way as to see it as God's work is to inquire into meaning.

---

6. Luther's *Die sieben Busspsalmen* (1517) as quoted in G. Helbig, *Theologie des Kreuzes* (Leipzig, 1933), 22; cf. WA, I (1883), 155, for the original title in full.

Index of Names

Aquinas, 140
Aretius, B., 102f.
Aristotle, 32ff., 39, 44, 56, 127, 140,
   146, 148, 150
Augustine, 109, 128, 141

Barth, C., 123
Bechert, R., 10
Berdyaev, N., 67
Berger, P., 39f., 49f.
Bernoulli, C. A., 113
Betti, E., 18
Bibrach, M. von, 31f.
Bloch, E., 124
Boniface, 36
Böschemeyer, W., 13
Buber, M., 83f.
Burkamp, W., 10

Calvin, J., 114
Caracciolo, A., viii
Clark, E. V., 18

Dux, G., viii, 18, 40

Ebeling, G., 104, 106

Eucken, R., 10

Fichte, J. G., 55
Fischer, B. B., 77
Feil, E., 4
Flake, O., 77
Frankl, E., 13ff., 76, 78, 93
Frege, F. L. G., 7
Freud, S., 13, 84ff.
Fromm, E., 120

Gadamer, H. G., 18
Galling, K., 22
Gebhard, W., 55
Gehlen, A., 40
Geis, E. R., 116
Gerhardt, P., 107
Gese, H., 125
Goethe, W., 61, 68, 130f.
Götze, A., 5
Gollwitzer, H., 56
Gomperz, H., 10
Grimm, I., 5
Grimm, W., 5, 62

Halbfas, H., 92

Index of Scripture References